I CAN'T

Coach Ron Brown's Search for Success

Arthur L. Lindsay

Cross Training Publishing
P.O. Box 1541
Grand Island, NE 68802

I CAN
COACH RON BROWN'S SEARCH FOR SUCCESS

Copyright © 1992 by Cross Training Publishing

ISBN 1-887002-01-4

Library of Congress Cataloging-in-Publication Data

Lindsay, Arthur L.
I Can / Arthur L. Lindsay

Published by Cross Training Publishing, Grand Island, Nebraska 68803

Distributed in the United States and Canada by Cross Training Publishing

Cover Illustrator: Jeff Sharpton
Printed in the United States of America

For additional books and resources available through
Cross Training Publishing contact us at:

P.O. Box 1541
Grand Island, NE 68802
(308) 384-5762

About the Author

Arthur L. Lindsay began writing for his hometown newspaper in Indiana while still in high school. During a varied career as a pastor, college administrator, missionary, and financial consultant, he has maintained his love for creative writing. He was a contributing author for *One Divine Moment*, published by Fleming Revel.

He is the father of four children: Tedrin, Timothy, Linda, and Colin.

This is what the Lord says:

"Let not the wise man boast of

his wisdom

or the strong man boast of

his strength

or the rich man boast of

his riches,

but let him who boasts boast

about this:

that he understands and

knows me,

that I am the Lord, who

exercises kindness,

justice and righteousness

on earth,

for in these I delight,"

declares the Lord.

Jeremiah 9:23-24

DISCLAIMER

Though this story is based upon a true account of Ron Brown's life, it seemed prudent to change the actual names of certain individuals in order to protect their right to privacy.

Contents

FOREWORD
BY TOM OSBORNE

• •

Ron Brown is truly one of the most unusual and remarkable people that I have met. Ron possesses a very strong work ethic. This was clearly illustrated to me when he was hired at the University of Nebraska as an offensive coach even though all of his previous experience as a player and coach had been primarily with the defensive side of the football. Ron worked diligently to become a receiver coach on short notice and made a remarkable transition. He continues to do everything that he can to further his abilities as a coach. In addition to his coaching abilities, he is a tireless and thorough recruiter. He consistently covers a large part of the United States in a very efficient manner for us.

More importantly, Ron has a tremendous compassion for young people. He spends a large portion of his summer running camps for underprivileged young people on the East coast, here in Lincoln, and also in Macy, Nebraska where he works primarily with Native American children. Ron has also been quite active in the Big Brother/Big Sister programs and always has extra time for our players and their personal needs.

Ron has a very strong Christian commitment. He sincerely tries to present himself as a living sacrifice in his service to Christ and is one who leads consistently by example. His faith is clearly evident in everything that he does as a coach, as a husband, and as a friend.

This book traces Ron's life from its inception at a foundling home in New York City to his childhood years on Martha's Vineyard to his career at Brown University as a student-athlete through several pro football camps and concludes with events involving his decision to go into coaching first at Brown University and later at the University of Nebraska.

This book is written in a way that enables the reader to really come to know Ron and, more importantly, the faith that motivates and inspires his life. Ron's efforts to become a professional football player provide insights into all that goes into a career in professional athletics that is not readily observable to the general public. Art Lindsay has done a fine job of putting all the information together in a very concise and readable form. I hope that you enjoy reading this book about a truly fine human being who inspires all of those who know him well.

INTRODUCTION
WHY THIS BOOK?

● ●

Ron and his wife, Molvina.

When Art Lindsay approached me with his desire to write a Christian biography based on my life, after listening to me present my testimony in 1989, I was very apprehensive.

My nature has normally permitted me to think that biographies should only be based on the lives of people, past or present, who are important and influential by the world's standards. The same would hold true in Christian circles. To read about a "household" name, such as Tom Osborne, seems appropriate; therefore, in a nutshell I was initially very embarrassed about a book written on my life.

But this is where my "normal" nature has failed me. Art convinced me that the book was about someone who in fact, was important and influential: Jesus Christ—not Ron Brown.

Ron Brown is merely a "worm on a hook." Hopefully, I'm bait for the great fisher of men, Jesus Christ. I was searching for success in this life, like almost everyone else—in all the wrong places. Until one day I met the Savior. That was the turning point in the game for me.

So how dare a basically unknown college assistant football coach comply with having a book written about him? The answer is that it isn't really about him. Rather, it's about the Lord Jesus Christ and how He can take a weak, needy, insecure, fearful, and doubting person like me—and transform that life into one filled with inspiration and purpose.

It is my desire that this book would inspire you to seek God's definition of success for your life. That is life's most thrilling victory!

Ron Brown
Assistant Football Coach
University of Nebraska

Chapter 1
THE RECRUIT WHO MADE THE TEAM

•••••••••••••••••••••••••••••

Sorrow etched itself deeply into the brow of Mike Stachmus. His nostrils objected to the terrible odor of hospital disinfectant. An awful awareness of his own limited ability and the despair of defeat flooded through his mind.

"How's the pain, son?" He asked, though he knew there was little he could do to relieve the discomfort of the weakened young man lying in the machine-shrouded bed next to him. Nor did he really expect an answer, for throughout the year-long physical ordeal, his son seldom had complained. Young Victor Stachmus was made of tough stuff. Physical agony was no stranger to him. In previous circumstances, however, it had been of his own choosing. He had knowingly accepted pain through strain as a standard for his life when he bridged the gap from childhood into adolescence. When he decided to compete in football he knew full well that pain was a necessary price to pay in order to excel.

Football was a natural decision for Victor. In his native Oklahoma every other endeavor paled in comparison to the college gridiron glories of the Sooners or the Cowboys. His earliest memories were of the excitement that his father and others reveled in as they argued pigskin tactics and strategy. Even as a kid, to him the mention of a wishbone had little to do with chicken. Vic was thoroughly infected from his youth with every aspect of the sport of football.

Of course his early football days were the simple joys of a sandlot game as his parents encouraged him without ever being pushy. However, as he entered his teens he began to take seriously his personal responsibility. He rigorously disciplined his growing body with the goal of becoming a standout player. Others could fall short of greatness, if they wanted to, by taking an easy road. He drove himself to pay the price in order to be the best.

Nonetheless, success in football was not an easy prize. He hoisted tons of weights, watched a thousand gut-grinding miles pass slowly beneath his feet, and slammed his body through endless hours of perfecting drills on the practice field. No tobacco. No drugs. No booze. No backtalk. He gave instant obedience to his coaches. His goal was specific: he would be the best football player that McAlester, Oklahoma had ever produced.

At the yet tender age of eighteen he attained that first plateau in his dream for life. His 6'5" frame, muscled with 250 pounds of never-say-die energy helped power his hometown to statewide prominence. He was a celebrated hero to all who knew him.

He was ready to begin the difficult climb to the next level of excellence: collegiate football. His prospects for an outstanding career were superb.

In football crazed Oklahoma such a young man, of course, was destined for notoriety in the university ranks as either an Oklahoma Sooner or an Oklahoma State Cowboy. That was a given. The choice was merely a decision between one of the two.

But it was impossible for the state to keep the youngster's talents hidden. His abilities attracted national media attention. Competition to sign him for a college football scholarship waged intense. Recruiters from across the nation took up residence on his doorstep. One such coach, Ron Brown from arch rival Nebraska, even had the audacity to head south to try to steal the prize. It was an improbable gambit: no Oklahoma athlete ever had gone directly from high school to play football at Nebraska.

Yet sometimes the unbelievable, the outrageous does happen.

Nearly everyone in Oklahoma who knew anything at all about football was in a state of shock when word got out that Vic had verbally committed to play college ball for the Big Red at the University of Nebraska. But Oklahoma State (OSU) did not give up the battle. The tug-of-war continued. Papers had not yet been signed.

Pressures built on the young man from many directions to reverse field. Most of his relatives were OSU fans. One high school teammate and close friend, Lee Keith, had committed to the instate school. College recruiters are fearless, resourceful, and forceful, or they don't last long, because competition for the best prospects is often fierce.

Yet, behind Victor's gentle outward demeanor was a resolve equally as tough as that of any coach.

The February signing deadline drew near. Oklahoma State increased its persuasive thrust. Ron Brown was off in Seattle visiting another high school standout, Jon Bostick. But Victor kept his word and held to his principles. He had made a commitment. He spoke his final word and stayed with his original decision, "I'm not changing my mind. Get these others off my back, Dad."

The excitement of the actual signing, with Coach Brown looking on, took place in February 1988. With that weighty matter behind him Victor turned his attention to the carefree pleasures of his final high school semester; and beyond that to the enjoyable rigors of his college career. He was really hyped up to wear a Cornhusker red jersey and play football at Nebraska. At the same time, however, he realized that the tiredness in his body was something other than the strain of physical exertion. The football season was long since over: he should have lots of pep. His strength always had been enormous: he could bench press 370 pounds five times consecutively and push away a half ton on the hip sled.

During the exhilarating days of his senior season he had brushed aside the infrequent, momentary inner pain. He simply challenged himself to tough it out and push ahead whenever he felt the drag of being unusually tired. But as spring burst forth in all of its beauty across the Oklahoma landscape he admitted to his parents that something must be wrong with him.

The shocking report after Victor's first visit to a doctor struck his family and friends a devastating blow. Nor could Ron Brown at first believe the distressing news he received from Victor's parents, Mike and Marianne. "Victor is gravely ill with acute lymphoblastic leukemia. His chance of living one year is one out of five. His chance of living five years is almost none."

Ron altered his schedule at once to fly to Tulsa to see Vic in the hospital. It would be but one of many such visits, for he considered commitment to be a two way street. The boy had committed to Nebraska, but Nebraska also was committed to the boy.

"Vic made a tremendous impact on me by the way he faced his battle with cancer" Ron commented at a sports banquet later. "Even through great physical pain and exhaustion he displayed incredible unselfishness and courage. He was always considerate and concerned, often asking me from his hospital bed, 'Coach, did you have a safe trip? Are you comfortable?'"

Victor maintained his composure amazingly well for a teenager. He never grumbled of physical distress to those attending him. On a pain tolerance scale of 0 to 10 he was usually at 8 or 9. He bravely bore the unbearable. As nurses asked, "How are you doing?", his customary response was, "Fine. I'm OK. I'm ready to go home."

The young man's previous health of body and his extreme enthusiasm for life gave him an early edge in the battle with leukemia. His condition improved dramatically after the first onset of the illness and the initial treatments. He was out of the hospital in 23 days; a near record time. He was able to attend his high school graduation, to a standing ovation as he crossed the stage.

The doctors told his dad that if Vic had a relapse his chances would be only 1 in 20 to survive a year. "I'm not telling Victor this," Mike responded angrily. "I've got more faith than that."

Shortly, however, Vic was back in the hospital. Again he responded to the medical treatment and was out in 28 days. He felt great and was doing fine. He knew he was going to win this one and he was preparing for college.

The cancer, though, stealthily built its forces for another onslaught. In September, when his blood count dropped again, he and his family were referred to specialists in Houston. Already he was missing what was to have been his first year of college football at Nebraska. In unfortunate contrast, however, he was playing the game of his life.

He was put on a new protocol with the hope that it would bring him back into remission for a bone marrow transplant which was his final hope. Mike Stachmus searched nationwide for a possible donor: there was only a 3/4 sibling match and there was no perfect unrelated match in the donor banks in the USA, England and the rest of Europe. No suitable match could be found. Victor was truly, one of a kind.

The spirits of all concerned sank low but refused to be beaten.

The Stachmus family was finally referred to the UCLA Medical Center in their determination to bring about a cure. New tests were conducted. The immediate results were most ominous. The cancer and the terrible side effects of the chemotherapy had devastated his vital organs. He was very weak.

The doctor was gentle yet blunt, "It's your decision. You can stay off chemotherapy and likely die in three weeks. Or you can go on heavy doses of chemo, with a fair chance that it'll cause organ failure, but with an outside chance that you'll make it through."

Victor didn't hesitate. One of his strongest attributes was that of being a possibility thinker, gaining advantage through positive action. "Let's get started," he responded with as much twinkle in his blue eyes as he could muster. "It's my last chance."

Unfortunately, the new protocol proved to be but an agonizing stalling tactic against the advancing enemy. Step by step the cancer kept marching forward throughout his system, claiming new ground with every passing hour. It was a monstrous war of attrition. Victor's strength continued to retreat noticeably day by day. His once robust body dwindled to, what was for him, a weak, tired, frail, and helpless shell of a mere 200 pounds.

Still, he made a tremendous effort to walk the halls twice a day to maintain his strength. But he had to stop. From the physical standpoint it appeared that the final battle was about to be engaged.

Thankfully, Victor and his family were not alone in their bid for victory. The young athlete's condition had been reported nationally in the press. That, along with the organization of a "Go Big Vic Day" in the states of Nebraska and Oklahoma, initiated a veritable flood of cards and letters from across the land. Thousands were standing in support of Vic and his family.

As Victor's physical war was drawing toward a dismal conclusion Ron Brown was attending the National Coaches Convention in Nashville, Tennessee. On the evening of January 8, 1989 about fifty coaches gathered together in a Fellowship of Christian Athletes prayer and share time during the convention. Several, including Brown, raised petitions to God for Vic Stachmus, praying that God would have his way with Victor both spiritually and physically.

Little did they know that at that very moment Victor was near death, fighting a debilitating battle, struggling fiercely with extensive internal disorders. The doctor, having done all he could, advised his parents, "There's a chance that Victor won't make it through the night. His blood pressure has dropped to 50 over 0."

Victor slept uneasily. He was afraid that he would soon lose his life. Because he didn't understand death, he feared it.

But as the coaches (and countless others across the nation) prayed for the All-American youth, Vic eased into such a restful slumber that those attending him dreaded that he had fallen into a finalizing coma. His breathing was shallow and labored. His blood pressure and vital signs were dangerously low. Nurses checked him every 15 minutes, certain that he would not make it through the night. Suddenly, unexplainably his condition improved. He awoke with a surprised smile on his face. Looking around the room and at his father and mother he stated in a bewildered tone, "Dad, I'm still here." His blood pressure had returned to 120 over 80 and his vital signs were stable.

Returning to sleep that evening, he had an amazing dream which he related to his relieved parents when he awoke brightly the next morning. "I walked up this beautiful avenue to the gates of heaven. There were brilliant lights beyond the entrance, so bright you couldn't see in. The guard asked me if I wanted to go in now or if I wanted to stay. The sight was very inviting, but I told them I wanted to fight it out. So they sent me back."

His father said, "Vic, you just had a dream."

But with an expression of total confidence he said, "No, Dad, I was actually there." He smiled lamely at his mother, "I guess you're stuck with me, Mom."

Marianne brushed her hand lovingly across his sunken cheek. "That's OK with me," she said as she choked back tears of comfort: her son was still here.

So, contrary to the medical odds, Victor was yet alive as the sun broke brilliantly through the Los Angeles haze on January 10. Obviously God's game plan for this star athlete was not quite finished.

Immediately after the conclusion of the convention in Nashville, Ron Brown flew to California to be with Victor. He marveled as to how quickly a potentially brilliant football career had screeched to a horrible halt. Expectations had been high. Not only that, but every contact with Victor had been a highlight for Ron in the previous year's recruiting effort. The muscular blond with the gentle blue eyes was on top of the world, the envy of all who knew him. Fame awaited. His powerful disciplined body, his finely honed innate athletic ability, his hard earned academic credentials, and his seemingly endless supply of energy all combined together to epitomize success to most Americans.

But Coach Brown wasn't going to UCLA to fret over what might have been. Rather he was on a specific mission. He realized that the end of life might be near for his college recruit. In a year's time the two had become closer than coach and athlete. They were good friends. Consequently Ron ached in his heart that there was nothing he could do to ease the excruciating experience of misery through which Victor was going. Notwithstanding, he did have one resource of power to share: his personal faith in Jesus Christ as Lord and Savior.

Not that the young coach had walked long with Christ himself. But he had come to relish that relationship with the Lord above all else. On the long flight to Los Angeles he meditated on an imaginary scene which most accurately illustrated to him his own decision for Christ.

He pictured himself at a three ring circus. Looking high above the sawdust, he sat spellbound in the big top as a tightrope artist walked across a forty foot stretch with just a pole for balancing. Nothing but "death defying" empty space lay between the performer and the hard packed ground thirty feet below. The man accomplished the amazing feat, over and back again. Ron and everyone around him clapped exuberantly. He then laid aside the pole and walked across the expanse, without a balancing support, pushing a wheelbarrow.

As he returned to the safety of his platform the applause rising from the stands was thunderous. "Fantastic! Unbelievable!" They roared.

The artist paused to look down upon his admirers in the audience. With a loud voice he asked, "Do you all believe that I can push this wheelbarrow across this narrow strand of wire with a person in it?"

Ron along with everyone else had seen him do so many great things that they all joined in a chorus of cheers. "Yeah, we believe that! We believe you can!"

The man's eyes swept slowly across the crowd. Suddenly Ron was startled to realize that the piercing stare had stopped directly on him. The gaze was dazzling and at the same time powerful. The masterful artist pointed down from his lofty perch and challenged the sturdy youth. "You! Ron Brown! Come on up and get in my wheelbarrow!"

In a sense that is exactly what happened with Christ. That concept had become the basic foundation for Ron's life. Nothing was more important to him than faith in Christ, entrusting himself continually to Jesus' care, getting in the Master's wheelbarrow. In doing so he had experienced for himself the gigantic difference between knowledge about God and faith in God, between mental awareness and heart belief.

Ron realized that Victor mentally knew about Christ. But had he ever gotten into the wheelbarrow? From the age of seven, when his mother's mother taught him his first prayer, Victor always prayed about truly important matters. Certainly he had turned to God many times during his ten months of physical suffering. Yet what he yearned for most he could not find. He had no inner peace. He feared death.

As his flight arrived in Los Angeles Ron had no plan as to how to talk to Victor about his relationship with the Lord. He wanted only that the young man know the satisfying thrill of being secure in Jesus' control.

On the ride from the airport to the Medical Center Ron prayed for wisdom. "Lord, I just dedicate this time to you. I don't know where Victor stands spiritually even though we've talked a little about it. A lot of people are wondering whether or not Victor will play football again. Some are wondering if he will live. I am wondering as to where he will spend eternity. Please, Lord, just use me. I've been on a tight schedule. I'm too tired and frazzled to handle this on my own."

As he arrived at the hospital, Ron was greeted warmly by Victor's mother and father. They had been keeping vigil through the long nights when death was supposed to have come at anytime, but somehow had been detained. Their spirits lifted noticeably at the sight of the man from Lincoln. Ron suggested that Vic's parents take a much needed break. "I want to have a few minutes alone with Vic anyway."

The boy had been so sick that he had been totally inactive, barely alert. He had slept all day long. But when Ron walked into the room he was awake, as if God had nudged him into consciousness for that very moment. He looked up in pleasant surprise, "Coach Brown!"

"Hey, Victor," Ron responded quietly, matching his somber tone with the hush that was upon the room. "Did you have a good trip?," Vic asked with a weak voice. "Are you comfortable?"

"Yes, I'm fine, Victor," the coach replied in admiration of the incredibly selfless attitude. Ron sat down next to the bed and took Vic's limp right hand in his. The boy's face was pale with a sick, greenish cast to it. He was quite apparently on death's doorstep: yet the door was still shut. The room was wrapped in stunned silence, the only sound came from a cart being wheeled down the hallway outside.

Searching for the right words, Ron finally asked, "Victor, what are you thinking right now?"

"Coach, I'm scared," he answered unashamedly, knowing he could trust the man beside him with such an intimate admission.

"Vic, there's not much I can do for you," Ron observed. "But would you like to pray?"

"Yeah, I sure do, Coach."

By the firm response, Ron understood at once that he didn't need to have any profound answers for Victor. God himself had prepared the boy's spirit for that particular instance. Ron opened the Bible he had carried into the room and said,"Vic, I want to read something to you from the Word of God first. I don't know where you stand with the Lord. But I do know what Jesus Christ accomplished in my life when I followed what it says here in Romans 10:9-13:

> If you confess with your mouth, 'Jesus is Lord.' and believe in your heart that God raised him from the dead you will be saved. For it is with your heart that you believe and are justified and it is with your mouth that you confess and are saved. As the Scripture says, 'Everyone who trusts in him will never be put to shame.' For there is no difference between Jew and Gentile - the same Lord is Lord of all and richly blesses all who call on him, for, 'Everyone who calls on the name of the Lord will be saved.'

"That's beautiful, Coach," Vic responded.

Ron closed the Book and said,"Vic, I believe that Jesus wants to indwell your soul right now. Do you believe that too?"

"Yes, I do, Coach. I want to accept Christ."

Ron pressed the issue a step further to make sure Vic understood clearly. "Do you want to receive Jesus Christ as your Lord and Savior?"

"I sure do, Coach."

"Well then," Ron suggested, "let's pray."

The two closed their eyes and talked to God. Ron's words flowed freely. Frequent communication with his Heavenly Father had become a natural part of his life. Vic, although in a weakened condition, searched for sincere words as he breathed out his repentance with difficulty. Holding the boy's practically lifeless hand in his, Ron was not certain during intermittent instances of silence whether or not Vic had maintained consciousness. However, as Ron finished praying he was stirred in his soul as he saw tears rolling down the young man's cheeks. God had truly touched his inner spirit.

Vic exerted himself to smile broadly at his mentor. He said, "Thanks, Coach! I feel great. I want you to know that I'm not afraid to die anymore. I'll never forget you." He paused for breath and continued, "I want a Bible. I want a whole Bible like yours."

"I'll go buy you one right away," Ron promised. He too felt great. He also was released into new strength. Just then Marianne came back into the room. Victor's voice seemed to pick up volume as he declared, "Mom, Coach Brown prayed with me!"

"I thought he probably would," his mother replied with an appreciative nod to Ron.

"And I asked Jesus to come into my heart—and I accepted him as my Lord and Savior."

"That's wonderful," his mother said admiringly as she stepped close to her son's bed to take his left hand in hers. Her face beamed with joy in seeing him so radiantly happy. "I've never felt like this before in my life," Victor continued excitedly. "My whole body...I could just feel something go over my whole body. I feel better than I've ever felt."

Tears welled up in Marianne's eyes. On the one hand she heard her son's ecstatic words but on the other she saw no physical change. She thought to herself, "Maybe he's being cured. It'll just be a slow steady process of getting well." She controlled her mounting excitement and kissed him on his cheek.

Later that afternoon Coach Brown delivered Vic's Bible and had prayer with him one last time before returning to his duties in Nebraska. His trip eastward, however, would not be with the uncertainty which had been his fretful foe on the trip west. By the gracious intervention of God, Vic had entrusted himself to Christ. He had boldly climbed into the wheelbarrow for a secure ride into the unknown beyond. Ron had written on the inside cover of the boy's Bible, "Victor accepted Jesus Christ as his Lord and Savior."

For ten months Mike and Marianne had snatched at every possible solution to bring their son back to health. It had been an agonizing strain on their emotions and physical stamina. Nonetheless, they had refused to give up hope, looking always to the prospects of the next day.

Victor's flush of excitement after receiving his assurance of peace in Christ brought renewed optimism to his parents. Marianne told her mother, "I want God to heal him!"

"I know you do, Marianne," her mother replied wisely, "but that may not happen. You're going to have to release him. All these people are praying for him, but you need to release him and let God do what he wants to do.

"I did that today," Marianne's mother confessed.

Making such a commitment of a son who had brought them nothing but pleasure for nearly two decades was not an easy decision for mother or father. They confessed to one another in a quiet moment, "It's just too hard to let him go."

On January 23, 1989, exactly one year from the day that she and her son had made his officially allowed visit to the University of Nebraska, Marianne let go. She drew up close to his bed and spoke in soft tones so as not to belie her underlying grief, "Victor, I've prayed for God to heal you. And I've asked God also to take you so you won't be in pain anymore. I've released you so that He can do whatever He wants to do." She bit hard into her lip to hold back the tears which wanted to flow.

"Victor," she concluded in resignation, "there's nothing else I can do. I've done everything I know." Victor's breathing was dry and shallow, "OK then," he said with difficulty, "I'm going to die. I have no fear of death."

His mother was heartbroken by his response. She put her head down on her arm on the edge of his bed and sobbed. With that resignation, Victor became exceedingly peaceful and closed his eyes to go to sleep. His parents' hearts began to spiral downward.

About fifteen minutes later Vic's eyes popped wide open. Once again he was totally alert. "Just talk to me, Mom," he pleaded with slurred speech. "Dad, I don't want you to think I'm a quitter, but I'm getting so tired."

"You're not letting us down, Son," his mother assured him.

"Hold my hand, Mom," he asked anxiously. "Don't leave."

"I won't, son, I'm right here."

Victor turned to his mother and said, "Mom, would you please ask Dad to leave."

Marianne got up and went over to Michael and said, "Victor wants you to leave, would you please go out in the hall."

His father left the room and sat in a chair in the hall by the door, not questioning why.

Victor turned to his mother and said, "Dad's not going to let me go. He'll want me to fight and to stay. And I can't." Marianne said, "Talk to your father, Victor. He loves you so much. He'll understand."

Marianne went into the hall and asked Victor's father to return to his bedside. Victor was having great difficulty in breathing and certainly in talking. He reached up with his large and gentle hands and put one on each side of his dad's head and pulled him within inches of his face. He looked at him and said, "Dad, we have fought too long, I'm tired and I want to stop. I want to ask your permission to stop fighting and to go on. I love you Dad."

His father's throat tightened. He gave permission with a nod of his head.

"Do you see heaven before you die?" Vic asked his mother.

"Some people do, some don't" she advised him as she brushed her reassuring hand across his brow.

Worriedly he said, "I've been trying to see it again like I did two weeks ago. I haven't been able to."

"Are you afraid?," she asked him.

"No," he replied simply. "I'm going to know some people in heaven...grandpa's there...and..."

"And I promise you," his mother interrupted, "I'll come see you someday."

"Thank you, Mom," he responded as he once again closed his eyes peacefully.

The night wore on slowly. There was a gentle hush on the room. Victor's breathing became calm and clear.

Mike left the room. His heart was breaking with anguish. He could not stand the pain of such uncertainty. He was not particularly thirsty but he drank again and again from the water fountain in the hallway near the nurses station—just a swallow at a time in nervous frustration.

Suddenly, after midnight he heard those feared words from Marianne; words which he had tried to push into oblivion. "Come quick!" She said. "Victor's calling you."

Mike rushed back into the room and sat at the foot of Victor's bed. A nurse held Vic's left wrist, monitoring his gradually ebbing pulse rate and then left, leaving Victor and his parents alone.

Victor was lying on his back and was having great difficulty breathing. His mother was exhausted and afraid and asked Victor in a quiet voice, "If you feel like you're leaving, let me know." He nodded in agreement. She laid her head on his chest and fell asleep with his arm across her back.

Suddenly, and very softly, with his eyes still closed, Victor started to gently rub his mother's head. He had done as promised. He woke her up.

Slowly, as if in recognition, with his eyes closed, his arms reached out to greet someone in an embrace. He raised slowly upward in bed, reaching out to someone who was coming to meet him. He stopped, then with a peaceful smile on his face, folded his arms across his chest and laid back down. With the Bible given to him by Ron Brown at his side, he made a quiet and graceful exit through the thin veil that separates this present life from the next.

It was 5:30 a.m. in Lincoln, Nebraska when Ron Brown was awakened with the anticipated, yet startling news from Marianne. His recruit was dead. Victor would never fulfill his dream of playing football for the Cornhuskers. But thankfully Ron had also recruited Victor Stachmus for God as well: and though he was a raw recruit of only a week he had made the team!

Chapter 2

SNATCHED FROM THE DUMPSTER

• •

Irene Chase enjoyed a life of wealth and luxury in the prestigious upper east side community of Grammercy Park in New York City. Through her husband's diligence and family fortune she never experienced in her own life the sufferings of hunger and homelessness which is the sad lot of tens of thousands in that expansive metropolis. Easily she could have insulated herself from even the awareness of such needs. Her money and position could have been a buffer against life as it is.

This elegant lady, however, was not of that nature. She was not caught up with everything she had. She deeply cared to know the needs of others. She stretched herself beyond the confining security of her exquisite home. She didn't need to experience the humiliation of being fed in a South Bronx soup kitchen to empathize with hunger pangs. She didn't need to freeze in a gutter in the Bowery in order to know that she was blessed in having a warm bed of her own. In spite of her great wealth of privileges she was yet sensitive to the pinch that others felt.

That very compassion, which was a driving force in her life, also created an inner strength which lent a particular grace to her already elegant beauty. In addition to her physical traits, the assurance by which she carried herself shined as a pure radiance, much as a rare diamond is admired when set in a particularly appropriate mounting.

Mrs. Chase chose never to flaunt her high position in the social register of New York's elite. For her it was a springboard by which she could plunge in to do her part to help cure some of the hurts of an aching world.

She had many interests throughout the city and beyond, but one particular work to which she devoted great energy and time and the resources of her own wealth was with the New York Foundling Home, located downtown on Third Avenue. She was a staunch ally of Sister Bernadette, director of the home, who took a passionate stand against the abortion option which was widely practiced even before the approval of the Supreme Court. Sister Bernadette was dedicated to providing every mother of every unborn child an alternative to the willful termination of a pregnancy. As chairman of the board, Mrs. Chase followed a determined course in working with Sister Bernadette who guided the day-to-day operation of the home.

The brownstone building, worn by decades of use and just as drab in appearance as all of its neighbors in the block, had served a host of occupants prior to becoming a refuge for unwanted children. The nuns had worked for years to get support and financing for their project of love; then nearly a whole year in renovating the facility. It was a happy occasion when the archbishop himself stood in the broad lobby to dedicate the home.

Yet, of far greater significance was the continuous line of frightened girls who, in time, entered through the large oak door to gain sanctuary. They were the purpose, after all, for which the home was conceived. Though they came from varied walks of life, they all had one thing in common. Each was carrying a child she could not keep.

Typical of the thousands who found their way to that always open door was Margaret Pearce, a lovely dark skinned music student from Tennessee. Her dream, in having come to the big city, was to become a success through study and serious effort. She intended to escape forever the difficulty of life in the South, which for a black girl in 1956 was heavy with ugly uncertainty. True to her goal, Margaret applied herself stringently to the rigors of study and performance. Her professors at the Manhattan School of Music gave her constant encouragement. She was without hesitation on her way up the ladder. Perhaps even stardom.

But even the best laid plans have a way of changing.

Arriving early one Sunday afternoon for a concert at the university, Margaret was impressed by the athletically built, well mannered young man who opened the door for her. He too was instantly aware of a particular charm in the statuesque young beauty from Tennessee. They had arrived separately but left arm-in-arm: two lonely hearts brought together in a strange city.

In the following weeks the two spent many happy times getting to know one another. He was fascinated by her carefree spirit, tempered by her strong dedication to a goal. She in turn loved the British tone of his deep throated accent. Also, his gentle concern for her every need nurtured a growing bond of affection.

Varheem had come from his native India to study engineering. He too was driven by a forceful ambition to succeed: a degree from Columbia University would assure him of both prestige and position in his home country. Therefore, when Margaret told him that she was pregnant he thought his whole world would crumble in on top of him. Instant fatherhood was not a part of his plan. He saw it as a tragedy. No way could a baby at this time fit into his future. Though he particularly loved the company of the beautiful young woman, taking on family responsibilities was, for him at that time, out of the question.

"Sister," Margaret said hesitantly when she first arrived at the Third Avenue brownstone five months later, "I'm not Roman Catholic. But I have nowhere else to turn."

Sister Bernadette welcomed her warmly, "My dear girl, come in, come in! We are all God's children. He has many flocks." The thin, energetic nun had assisted hundreds of other young women through the particularly trying ordeal of being an unwed mother. As she observed Margaret she was only sorry that this one had waited so long before seeking help. It was obvious that she would soon give birth.

It was a sad time for the expectant mother. Her lover had found cause not to return to the University for the fall term. His decision came at a time when she needed him the most. She had been able neither to work nor to continue her studies. But most distressing of all, she felt alienated from her family. That was not through their neglect or rejection. She simply had not possessed the courage to tell her mother of her plight. She dreaded to bring shame to those she loved so deeply. At the same time she was afraid of being turned away by her family as she had been denied by Varheem: to whom she had entrusted herself. She could not face a hurt like that again. Better to suffer alone, she decided, than to face another rejection.

Bravely, Margaret had undertaken for herself until the burden within her became too great. But once established in the home she sensed an immediate acceptance because everyone was engaged in fighting the same struggle as she. They understood the agony of bringing a new life into the world without a husband's support. They all shared the same sorrow of having no one who cared to press a loving hand against a stretched abdomen to feel the little life on the inside kicking like a football player. The nuns and other young women became Margaret's family. Her consolation. As she was their's. With renewed determination she knew she'd make it.

Nonetheless, it was a nostalgic time for all the young women in the home as Thanksgiving Day drew near. Friends may mean a lot, but holidays are a special time for family. Margaret longed to be with her mommy in Tennessee. To hear that tender voice. To eat her good cooking. But especially to feel the gentle caress of her consoling arms. Margaret felt she had little about which to be thankful that cold November Thursday. "I am too sick to eat," she complained to Sister

Bernadette."But worse. I'm afraid. This child is coming soon. I had my first real labor pain this morning."

"Now, don't you be afraid," Sister assured her. "We've been through this more times than I can possibly remember. We'll be right here with you through it all."

"No, you don't understand," Margaret said, with sorrow in her dark brown eyes. "I'm not afraid for myself. I'm afraid for the child. I won't be around when it needs me. Will it understand why its mother and father deserted it at birth? This child is a part of me. I love it! And I don't want it be as alone as I've felt in the last six months."

The normally composed nun bit her inner lip to squelch a tear that wanted to respond to expressed sorrow.

"Now, my dear girl," Sister Bernadette said, with a strong tone of assurance she resurrected from her reserves, "I'll see to it that the baby is placed with just the right family. Through the adoptive parents it'll gain a double understanding of love. First, that you loved it enough to give him life rather than death. And second, that they loved it enough to choose it special."

Margaret was little comforted. She smiled only in humble submission.

On November 28, 1956, the solemn silence of the New York City Foundling Home was pierced by the loud wail of a new voice, announcing his traumatic arrival in God's world. A strong, energetic boy burst into life. Delighted to be there. His mother had chosen to allow God's plan for life to not be interfered with. No oblivion in a rusty dumpster for him. Four days later Margaret held her little boy for the last time. She was headed back to Tennessee, to her mother."Son," she said to the bundle of potential cradled in her arms, "please always remember that I love you with all my heart."

Tears rolled down her cheeks as she walked along Third Avenue, suitcase in hand, to the subway. She never looked back. But she would never forget that little boy who would never know her. She would always celebrate November 28 as a day of joy: she had made the right decision.

Though Sister Bernadette had assured the young woman that she would see to it that the child would be placed in just the right home, she knew from the beginning that it would be difficult. Most of the potential adoptive parents in New York were white; and in the mid-1950s few were looking to break the color barrier. There was little demand for black babies, even a little charmer like this one. And the sorry fact that he had been born with a clubbed foot complicated the case even more.

At the first meeting of the Board of Governors of the home after Christmas, Sister Bernadette drew attention to this particular problem. "More and more, the young ladies who come to us are from the black or Hispanic communities. Yet rarely do we have a request for such a child. This darling little boy has been in our care now for six weeks and I have no one looking to take on such a responsibility."

"I have an idea," Irene Chase said in immediate response. "My groundskeeper at my summer home on Martha's Vineyard would be a perfect father for the boy. He and his wife are childless. This would fill a great void in their lives as well."

"But, Madam, that's out of state," one man objected. "That's unheard of. We can't send children out of New York."

"Nonsense!" Mrs. Chase dismissed the disagreement authoritatively. "We have a child who needs a home: and Arthur and Pearl Brown have a home that needs a child. That sounds like a perfect match to me. We'll just have to find a way to change the rules."

"You say Mr. Brown is a groundskeeper?" Another board member asked. "Can such an income support a family? Especially one with a growing, handicapped little boy."

"Having the love of a hard working father is more important than having a wealthy one," Mrs. Chase responded. "And I ought to know because my father was both. But I respected him far more for his diligence than for his riches.

"Arthur Brown is most certainly a worker. Besides

gardening for me and others, he serves as a garage attendant, and does night jobs, sweeping out shops. His wife Pearl also works as a maid and a cook."

"I assure you, Madam, they sound like fine people," the vice chairman admitted. "But how do we convince them that they need a baby in their busy lives?"

"Mrs. Brown and I've talked about it a great deal," Mrs. Chase responded. "For years she and her husband have longed to have children but couldn't. I believe if we advise them of this need and opportunity they would be very happy to have an addition to their family at last."

On Mrs. Chase's strong recommendation and insistence the board finally approved for her to contact the Browns. The couple was surprised by the suddenness of the opportunity and at first were a bit hesitant, at forty years of age, to take on a new lifestyle as parents. However, they quickly warmed to the idea and became eager to at last be able to satisfy the unfulfilled dream of their lives.

"We would love to have the boy," Arthur Brown informed Mrs. Chase, "if there is any way you can cut through the red tape for us to bring him to Massachusetts."

Irene Chase enjoyed the challenge of blazing a new trail. It was like giving free reign to a thirsty horse with a stream of cool water beyond a distant hill. She took to the task with relish. Certainly setting a precedent is never easy. That is true even more so when it involves the political and conflicting rights of two state governments. The system did not want to budge. But Mrs. Chase and others were not easily discouraged. They pushed on with relentless perseverance.

For Pearl and Arthur Brown the waiting and uncertainty seemed as difficult as going through childbirth. Indeed the process continued on through the winter, the spring, and into summer; eight months in all. But, as always, persistency won the victory.

In August the Browns proudly carried their almost-ready-to-walk son out of the New York City Foundling Home and headed for the sun-bathed haven of Martha's Vineyard. The months of delay had given Pearl Brown many anxious thoughts as to whether she could ever genuinely feel that the child was hers. However, after only five seconds of holding the tiny, helpless life in her arms all doubts were gone. She adored the little boy with all her heart. Lovingly she touched the heavy, black, backward shoe on his left foot. It was awkward, but was intended to correct his problem. She was certain it would do just that. She wanted total health for her child. She was his mother.

It was a lofty day for the middle aged couple when their son was christened Ronald Arthur Brown. Their expectations for him were high.

Chapter 3

DANCE ALL YOU WANT, BUT DON'T STOP TO SLEEP

• •

Most people have no idea where Martha's Vineyard is. A few politically minded individuals recall the questions, mystery, and controversy surrounding the bizarre incident of Ted Kennedy and the death of Mary Jo Kopekna at Chappaquidick. And movie buffs recall it as the picturesque location for the filming of the shock thriller "Jaws".

But for Arthur and Pearl Brown and the pride of their lives, their newly adopted son, it was home.

Vineyard Haven, six miles directly across Vineyard Sound from the Massachusetts' mainland, had been refuge to Pearl Brown's family for two generations. Her ancestors, seeking a new beginning, modestly settled in the village when they first emigrated to the United States from the Cape Verde Islands, off the northwest corner of Africa. Throughout the trials of establishing an identity in a strange land, her relatives had held together in a closely knit bond. Consequently, within a four block area from the house to which she and her husband brought their infant son were dozens of cousins and uncles and aunts.

The comparatively small, 120 square mile island of Martha's Vineyard stands as a calm guard against the raging Atlantic Ocean along Massachusetts' southern approach. Its quaint, quiet way serves as a permanent home to about 12,000 residents. But it also became a favored playground for rich and sometimes rowdy vacationers even before the turn of the century. Its normally tranquil population is overrun by five or six times as many vacationers during the gorgeous sunshine months of summer. The pristine, unspoiled waters are special attractions. In addition to other aquatic sports, they afford magnificent sailing opportunities which attract yatchsmen as surely as fish take to bait.

With no landbridge to the mainland, the island is somewhat isolated, accessible solely by air and boat. The ferries which ply the waters regularly for the tourist season taper off markedly during the long, unhurried winter months. Accordingly, the widespread communities of Martha's Vineyard have been able to maintain a considerable bit of their Nineteenth Century charm. It is a great place to live and do as you please, if you're not looking for grand cultural activities.

The people who live there all year are primarily vocational, blue collar workers. There is little hubbub of high powered business, no university crowd, and only one high school. Many of the kids who grow up on the island never leave it permanently. They stay, parenting another generation. In most all respects it was a great place for Arthur and Pearl Brown to rear their son (and daughter Theresa whom they retrieved from the New York Foundling Home a year later). The quiet manner and slow pace of the island for nine months of the year was in perfect keeping with their own old fashioned attitude of hard work matched with personal integrity.

It was at an early age, with parents old enough to be his grandparents, that Ron built an orderly attitude toward relationships. His first concern, insisted on by his father, was obedience to his parents. He saw it as a duty to live up to the high expectations his mother and father set for him. Their standard was simple: stay drug free, alcohol free, and do well in school. Though his parents never finished their own formal education they expected their son to be an "A" student. To help keep his son on track Arthur Brown enforced a strict curfew of no week nights out and no weekend late nights.

Ron did not rebel. He recognized the love behind the plan and even took pride in it: many parents didn't care that much. Nonetheless, like any other action oriented youth he wanted desperately to hang out with the other kids and be their friend.

"Ronny, you're a square," his cousin Zachary said harshly as they were walking home from school one day. "You don't drink. You don't get high and hang out at night. You don't even have a steady girl."

"What would I do with a steady girl?" Ron thought sadly to himself as he turned his back and walked away without arguing. "Take her to church?" For church was the one other expectation that his parents insisted on for him. They saw to it that he never missed a week at mass.

To compensate for the great gulf that existed between what his mother and father demanded and what his peers enticed him toward Ron developed a self-righteous attitude. "Hey, I'm on God's side." He thought. "I have it all together. I do well in school and I'm becoming a good athlete because I come from a disciplined home." He proudly looked down on the other children because their lives didn't reflect the same regulated lifestyle as his.

Nevertheless, he was lonely. He recoiled at being called a coach's pet or a teacher's pet. Such taunting is hard to take when you're in junior high. He insulated himself in two ways. Inwardly, where no one could see, he kept his emotions to himself. Outwardly, where most of the emphasis of success in this world was focused, he began to build an image by involving himself heavily in sports. It was a great way to escape the negative charge of being a square—and also, fortunately, he was good. He had outgrown the clubbed foot with which he had been born and was endowed by his Creator with definite agility and grace.

In addition to the peer pressures, felt by any maturing young person, there were built-in difficulties for Ron in facing the underlying inequalities of the island's social fabric.

Racism was not an often mentioned issue within the white community. They were comfortably in control. But the ugliness of prejudice was a continual menace to the black minority. That ignorant monster was always hovering just out of sight, waiting to pounce. His parents had learned to live above the verbal and nonverbal insinuations of inferiority: slights from some whites did not bring them down. Instead they concentrated on building self respect by adhering to their own high value system of doing their best in everyday work. Besides, they had seen dramatic improvement toward racial equality in their lifetime. Their northern community of the fifties was outwardly far advanced to what changes the Deep South was only beginning to experience.

But a new day was yearning to dawn, to shed new light in dark places. With it Ron's generation began to stretch into maturity for itself. He and others his age had to make their own stand in life as it is and possibly push it into becoming life as it ought to be. In this regard, the struggle of young blacks for a wholesome identity always has been an intense battle because of the insensible prejudice so often blocking their path.

No matter how much encouragement and support he got at home, however, Ron realized early on that he had to make a place for himself in a subtly hostile world. Why did the color of his skin make a difference to so many people? He was a nice looking kid, respectful of his elders, got good grades, was fast on his feet, and quick with his hands. But he learned from his earliest contacts outside the black community that he had to be much better than a white just to be taken seriously, to have an equal chance. Life at home, however, helped him overcome many of those harsh, negative realities of the world in which he lived. His parents were not influential people. They did not have a lot of money or earthly possessions. But they held high demands for their children always to do their best.

Arthur Brown did not have a philosophy of "let's reason together and talk this through." It was more like, "let's get it done!" No questions asked. Such a no-nonsense standard worked to Ron's favor. In following his dad's example, at an early age, he developed a satisfying pride in doing a job right.

That kind of attitude was in striking contrast to the mentality of the two principle tourist types which flocked like migrating birds to the tiny island resort area during the high season months. First, there were those of the obvious wealthy, flashy, jet set breed. With too much easy money and too little incentive to expand their horizons or exert themselves unnecessarily in self-improvement, they tended to depend on others for effortless entertainment.

Then too, the pleasures of the sand, sunshine, and surf of the Atlantic were a natural attraction for those who considered themselves to be upwardly mobile. These workers of the middle-class thought it necessary not only to drive a Mercedes and send their kids to the "right" schools but also to vacation at the "right" spot. But at best, whatever reason either type had for coming, the magnificent scenic wonders of Martha's Vineyard satisfies such fast movers only in the daylight hours. The splendid quiet can become boring after a time. Consequently, along with carefree vacationers, a host of pros also flood in every summer to fill that dull, inert gap. They provide lively entertainment and enjoyment through the evening and into the wakeful night hours.

Eddie Heywood, well-acclaimed after World War II for his refreshing touch of jazz music, was one of the more popular of the performers who included the Martha's Vineyard night spots on his itinerary year-after-year. His outstanding rendition of his gold record signature song, "Canadian Sunset", kept him as a top draw for a decade. His mellow music was in perfect keeping with the laid back pace of the seaside oasis. Everyone, regardless of race, was proud to call him friend. He was favored by countless name droppers.

Eddie Heywood was a bridge between black and white.

After years of returning to the island for summer stints Eddie decided that there was no other place in his wide travels which he liked more. He figured that it was time to establish roots. He searched diligently for days and finally found a house which suited his desires perfectly. He put down his deposit and began preparations to take possession.

That's when the bottom fell out of the love affair between the entertainer and many of those he had entertained. The house chosen by the popular black musician was smack dab in the middle of a well-to-do white section of town. The "boy" had overstepped his bounds. Whites were willing to dance to his music but not when he piped a block busting tune. "Sing all you want," they advised indirectly, "but don't think you can sleep in the house next door."

The white community was enraged. Tensions ran high. Though Heywood got his house, the long struggle rekindled strong emotions which had been hidden for years. The white majority gave in only grudgingly.

The confrontation had a lasting impact on Ron Brown, who was a good friend to Heywood's son, Robert. How do you explain color barriers to a growing boy with a zest for life? Were his opportunities in the world limited? He and his friends saw an evil and were angry. They were stuck on an isolated island, controlled by unwritten yet definite restrictions. They were filled with life's questions and there were no intelligent answers in sight.

So, while still in grade school Ronny was fully aware of two facts: not only was he considered "different," but there were two distinct communities on his small island home. Though he experienced no physical violence, the insidiousness of prejudice was impossible for him to comprehend. He could not help but wonder if he would ever attain success in this world. Yet that flame burned brightly in his heart.

Another factor which contributed heavily to the boy's early psychological development was the fact that he himself was not Cape Verdean. All of his adoptive cousins could boast of a pure, direct lineage across the expanse of the Atlantic to their roots. He could not. "Ma, they just don't accept me as part of the family—because I'm different."

"Nonsense," his mother would assure him, "of course they do."

However, she never convinced him.

Fortunately though he had other interests which kept him occupied. After outgrowing the awkwardness of the clubbed-foot of his early childhood, his natural agility and athletic ability began to push him ahead of the competition. With that to his advantage, Ron built a strong comfort zone for himself where he was certain he could excel—in sports.

Though his greatest combination of talents added up to a promise of success in football, there was not much of an opportunity on the island. Martha's Vineyard Regional High School was too small to compete significantly with teams on the mainland. So basketball became the primary rallying point for the school's athletes and fans alike. At least that was true for the white end of town. They knew that their kids had a lock on the starting positions. In grade school Ron and his friends contented themselves with perfecting their skills on the public playground. For hours on end they played four-on-four half court, pausing only for an occasional shouting match about a rule infraction or elbowing one another for a turn to take gulps of refreshing water at the single pipe water fountain.

The summer before Ron's seventh grade, however, circumstances in that small corner of the sporting world took a dramatic turn. A new coach, Jay Schofield, came to the island to take responsibility for the sport fortunes on Martha's Vineyard. The "good ole boys" days came to an end. Schofield, who was white, was a no nonsense type of coach who looked for character and determination as well as skill in an athlete. He spent hours every day during that summer of 1970 both observing and occasionally competing with youngsters on the outdoor basketball courts. When school started the coach singled Ron out, "I've been watching you play. You're good. I hope you'll try out for the team when you're a ninth grader because you have potential to be a very good athlete—and, from what I hear, a good student as well.

Those words naturally pricked the fancy of the thirteen year old kid, but his friends were not impressed. "You're not going to listen to that honky, are you? He's not interested in you. He doesn't care about you. He just wants to win games for his own hide."

Nonetheless, bursting with just as much desire to succeed in life as he was endowed with physical prowess, Ronny did listen. He showed up for tryouts at the start of the ninth grade basketball season. It was a significant first step for him on the long road of competitive sports. Fortunately he was not a "token" black. In Schofield's first two seasons the color barrier slowly faded and dissolved as the black guys dominated the court.

Again prejudice tried to rear its hideous head. "Why have you given the starting role to black boys and benched our sons?" Some of the island's majority cried.

"Because they're better players," the coach answered matter-of-factly. "All summer long while the whites were at the beaches trying to improve their tans the black guys were busy improving their basketball skills on the practice courts. If you don't believe me, watch the progress of this team during the season."

His claim was prophetic. Martha's Vineyard High School ceased being considered an easy victory by schools on the mainland. Under a dedicated coach the players too became dedicated. Consequently the fans took the change of lineup without further whimper. The complaining stopped. Nothing like a positive won/lost record to undergird a coach's right to call the shots.

With guidance from Schofield, a man for whom he gained undying respect, Ron took to the rigors of organized sports with an unquenchable enthusiasm. His autumns were consumed with football, the winters followed with basketball, and he filled the intervals with more of the same. With only twenty-three players on the Martha's Vineyard football team Ron was called on by Coach Gerry Gerolamo to play several positions: quarterback, receiver, safety. Whereas for basketball he was normally a floating guard. Though Ron had built-in strength, stamina, and skills, Coaches Schofield and Gerolamo stressed and insisted on mastering fundamentals— that too was an attraction to the teenager whose dad had always inspired him to aim for perfection.

Ron loved everything about athletics. There was the thrill of running a drill a hundredth time, then finally realizing that it had become almost second nature. The gasping for air and a burst of sweat when suddenly a second wind kicks into gear from out of nowhere. The joy of reversing field so expertly that the last defender between you and the goal is faked out of his socks as you speed on your way to score. The adoration of fans in the stands which spreads into instant recognition and status on the street. The sweet taste of success after snatching victory from the jaws of defeat, or after a loss making a promise, "we'll rock'em next time". That love in Ron Brown for anything related to sports produced results. The would-be athlete, although not physically the most talented in his high school, used the combination of character and talent to become an area star in both basketball and football.

Arthur and Pearl Brown followed the exploits of their son with devotion, making dozens of ferry crossings to the mainland season after season so as not to miss a single contest in which he competed. By the onset of his senior year in high school he had earned a statewide reputation and was of definite collegiate material. Scouts from eastern seaboard universities began making overtures to recruit him for basketball and football. As the year progressed he had two difficult choices to make: which sport and which school.

Though basketball had gotten him into competitive athletics, Ron realized that his greater natural talents were in rough and tumble football. It was a tough decision to lay aside the joys of one sport to concentrate on another; but with the final nod going to football the selection of a college was easy. From the outset of the first recruiters pounding on his door Ron had fancied one school above all the others. When commitment day rolled around he signed with Brown University in the Ivy League.

Shortly before leaving home to start his college career a respected lady of the community asked him to make one other commitment. "Ronny," Mrs. June Farmer said, "you have been such a good boy. Such a positive role model. You go to church every Sunday. You do all the right things. It seems we all want our kids to be just like you. I want you to make a promise to me."

"Sure, Mrs. Farmer," Ron replied seriously, "anything. What would you like me to do. I'll do anything for the older people in the neighborhood."

She answered, "Well, I would like for you to go to church every Sunday when you get to college. You know, so many young boys when they go to college, or when they go off somewhere else forget all about their upbringing."

A smile of relief creased the teenager's face. He had feared that the old friend of his mother was going to lay some heavy cause on him which would have hampered him in making a name for himself at Brown. But he could take church in stride and not miss a step in a triumphant march to college success. He had big plans for himself once he escaped the island. He was on his way. College scouts had found him. Next it would be the pros. Ron Brown had been put down enough. He had seen too much of racial suppression. He would help change things. He was going to succeed in this world. Church was the least of his concerns.

"Yes, Ma'am!" Ron replied with pleasure. "That's easy. I'll do that. I like going to church!"

Chapter 4
THE BIG SPLASH

● ●

Twin ambitions stirred excitement in the heart of the energetic, but as yet unproven young athlete as he headed for an unknown adventure on the campus of Brown University. Ron could not have defined or distinguished between those two desires, for they were part and parcel with one another. Football was what he intended to use to build prestige and gain success. But equally important to his famished spirit was the new freedom by which he could fashion a new image.

In fact, the latter was such a driving force that it had priority. Even though athletics had been a key factor in helping lift him from a relatively poor home to a promising opportunity at a major academic institution, he was most anxious to gain popularity among people his own age. He longed to fill the empty void of loneliness which had overshadowed his teenage notoriety like a rain cloud at a summer's picnic. Even when he had been showered by praise and admiration he had felt unfulfilled, alone, and isolated.

It's true that Ron Brown had much for which he should have been thankful and satisfied. During four years of consistent effort in high school he had achieved academic excellence: he applied his quick mind willingly, eagerly to study. In athletics he earned a statewide reputation as an outstanding competitor, zealously committing himself to tough training and giving heed to his coaches. And, if that were not enough, he was highly respected in his community for his moral lifestyle. Yet, it was not enough for Ron. He was not satisfied within himself.

By all normal standards for a high school graduate he was a well qualified success. Nonetheless, Ron Brown was restless. He was bursting with pent up desires to achieve unrealized adventure. His urge to expand his universe was ripe for anything, everything the world had to offer.

In reality Ron was little more than a kid, eighteen years of age, when he first exploded onto the college scene in September, 1975. Like most all other freshmen, at a thousand different schools, he wanted people to think he was dynamic. However, within himself he felt more like a spent firecracker, which translated into initial shyness. He was still trying to come to grips with who he understood himself to be as a person. The struggle of course had been going on for a long time. It was suddenly aggravated by transplantation two hours away from all the familiarities and securities of home. His emotions were in turmoil. In all his learning no one had taught him, nor did he know how, to assess the conflicting aspirations and attitudes of the underdeveloped individual who inhabited his well developed body. For years he had received high marks of praise from older people. Great! But he had never fit into the standards by which friends his own age lived. There was an awesome void between those two opinions and he decided on a scheme by which he could straddle the chasm.

"The island is two hours away. I can still please those older people at home," he determined to himself. "I can still make them think that I'm such a good little boy, who grew up, and is a fine upstanding man. But, now that I'm in a new place, I can develop a new identity, a new Ron Brown. So I can go ahead and be a class clown. And maybe I can try some of those devious things most of the other high school people did and I didn't. Maybe I can be popular among my friends and still be respected by people back home."

It was an impossible stretch: with one foot firmly planted

in the past on Martha's Vineyard, and the other attempting to find a secure foundation in the present in Providence, Rhode Island.

The first test of his resolve came within a few days of freedom away from the authority of home. He willingly had made a solemn vow to Mrs. Farmer never to succumb to the temptation to sleep in on the sabbath. Faithfully, self-righteously he slipped out of the slumbering dorm that first Sunday morning. He went to church, as had been his family's standard from his youth. Sitting there through the service though he realized that the guys he hung around with on the football team were nowhere to be seen. Others he had met were just as obvious by their absence. Scanning the congregation of strangers he began to feel very out of place. "This isn't any fun," he said to himself. "My new found friends aren't here. It was all right back home with mom and dad because it was good for my standing around town. But here I don't have a reputation. Not yet! And this isn't the image I want to develop."

What a splash! Not even a week had passed before the normally responsible youngster let one foot go kerplunk! It slipped off the familiar security of Martha's Vineyard and into the water nearer the mainland. Seemingly just a small step. It was insignificant by itself. Yet, who can gauge the value of even one broken promise. Would there be others?

For Ron that was it. He set a new course. No more wasted time in church for the newly emancipated Mr. Brown. True, there were no immediate disastrous consequences. Though the waves of the splash washed clear to the shores of heaven, no one in Providence either noticed or judged him harshly for his change of direction. Indeed, no one bothered even to know or care that he had tripped.

The great splash, however, that hundreds did observe and openly appreciate was in the succeeding days when the ambitious and friendly young man began to make his presence known across the breadth of the Brown University campus. He was free. Enthusiastically he extended himself into every possible opportunity for social exposure. From the football field to the dormitory to the parties—and even in the halls of learning—the "I Can Kid" from the quaint offshore island was sought after wildly and was welcome in the best cliques.

In high school he had contented himself with the confining privilege of having one steady girl. After all, with the restrictions his parents had laid on him his romantic options on Martha's Vineyard had been extremely limited. But with his sudden new freedom of choice he determined to make up for lost time.

The response was an enormous boost to the young man's ego. There was no shortage of open doors for him. His apparent wholesomeness was an attraction, especially when matched with a sometimes wild dash of daring. He was clean—cut and handsome, with an angular face, and lean athletic build. Some thought as well that they themselves gained status just being with him. All of that was a heady new experience for the formerly quiet kid from a sheltered background.

By all outward appearances Ron handled the new variety of worship well. He managed to maintain his composure for public consumption. However, in times alone he worried that the days of adoration someday would escape him and he would be left only with his nagging fear of inadequacy. Often he was at cross purposes with his own emotions. Yet, he brushed aside the concerns in order to relish every minute. He had arrived.

Due to Ivy League rules, Ron's playing time was limited to the freshman team, and it was satisfying enough to him to be a starter. He gained invaluable experience, gearing himself for a varsity starting position as a sophomore.

His first semester in college consequently flew by him like a whirlwind. He was caught up happily in the frenzy of nonstop activities in which more often than not he was a central figure. The acclaim of his fellow students was such a boost to his ego that he freely allowed events and opinions to dictate his schedule and actions. Little by little he surrendered control of his own course. New friends, and his own imperfect design of a new image, brought relentless demands upon him. Ron was under the impression that he was free just because things were different. In reality he was allowing decisions to be made for him by the pressures and plans of others.

Temptations which had been held at bay by the strict standards of his parents exerted themselves against even his best instincts. The liberated teenager muddled along. He flowed compromisingly within the intensity of group dynamics. How much could a little bit of sin hurt?

Further, in conformity to the portrait of the new Ron Brown he was trying to paint, he also decided that he needed to slack up some in his efforts for the coaches and profs. In the university setting of the Seventies it was not in style to be the teacher's pet. No more front row seat in the classroom with an attentive look: slouching in the back with a whispered joke was more certain to gain the attention of classmates. Sure, he'd play hard on the gridiron because he enjoyed it, but extra laps and 110% stuff just to gain favor with a coach was taboo. He would get by on his ability.

Nevertheless, in spite of his experimentations, Ron somewhat imagined that he was deviating more from the strict standards of his past than was actual fact. The twig of his life had been so bent by the loving concern of his mom and dad that there was an inner safety mechanism which limited how far afield he could possibly let himself go. Certainly his folks would have been appalled to know he had allowed his guard to slip so low. But just as Ron had headed for college with two primary goals for himself (image and football) there were two far more powerful forces at work in his behalf. A divine plan had marked him, as it does every person in the world. And the hunger of his own spirit would keep him famished for truth until he found it.

Though new acquaintances, activities, and attitudes signaled a detour from his prior path, Ron's character was only marred, not destroyed. From his earliest years there was a definite, obvious imprint on his spirit which demanded greatness. It would take more than a round of frat parties with the temptations of alcohol and too many girls to rend his heart from its foundation. He had seen too much degradation and senseless racial prejudice to lose sight of his heartfelt goal. He had within him from his youth a desire to make a difference in this world. That was a constant focus. Especially he sensed he was destined to be a witness of excellence both in and for the black community. That inner resource, raw and though as yet unrefined as it was, withstood the storm.

More importantly, also, there was a divine scope for his life. Surely his birth mother had sensed something special within her when she determined to give him life rather than a brutal end in a hospital dumpster. Pearl Brown also knew she was holding a child with purpose as she carried her little club-footed darling out of the foundling home. And though unseen, God was continually in control in spite of the fact Ron Brown was unaware of it. True, he had made a big splash when he landed on campus. Many would remember him for years. But the immersion of true importance was yet to come.

Chapter 5
TARGETED
•

Ron Brown was not unique. There were many other young men just like him, with similar traits of high energy, eagerness, and daring. Yet, not everyone at Brown University in the 1970's was in that mold. Not all were hung up on football, infatuated with girls, and determined to find instantaneous personal gratification. In fact, a definite majority was dedicated to the Ivy League tradition of pursuing academic excellence. Regardless of the obvious sacrifice of temporary pleasures, they were determined above all else to gain knowledge. That keen awareness of purpose on the part of the faculty and most students was what kept Brown University near the top of the list of every high school guidance counselor in America as "highly competitive". Significantly, an education received there should qualify a graduate of the institution for further doors of opportunity.

Indeed, for the small army of academicians on the campus, learning was an end in itself. Dialoguing with one another within the bounds of the stately campus on the outskirts of the city was all the thrill they sought or thought. Pitting their minds in a good game of chess or quietly consuming the contents of a good book were to them more worthy challenges than competition in any sport, football included. They viewed such rugged endeavor at best as a mere physical venting of energy for those whose attention to more proper and essential pursuits was totally inadequate. Such students tended to lonely test tubes in the laboratories and gathered quietly in the small study rooms near the back of the library. Their most treasured enjoyment was in dedicating themselves to further insight by means of research and reasoning.

However, for the majority, the typical, run-of-the-mill student, long hours of study was not necessarily a pursuit of pleasure. It was a necessity in order to match the stiff test of minds at such a major center of learning. Yet they also realized that academics had to be modified with some ordinary relief. Brown might be considered boring to a visitor from a "country club university", yet pizza is still the campuswide food of preference and modern rock the concert of choice. The majority of students are identical to those found in any other college—a blend of youthful vitality from across the American landscape, with a healthy smattering of internationals to produce a true cosmopolitan influence.

Additionally, as in most other late Twentieth Century universities, there was a vibrant minority which followed a different agenda. Though they attended Brown to get a first rate education and ate pizza and liked football and enjoyed dating and social gatherings, they had an overriding allegiance to a Higher Power. They were convinced that the key to success was a truly well-rounded life, beginning with a vital spirit. Others might have been out of balance with too much emphasis on strain-training the brain at one extreme or excessive exercising of the body on the other. But these young people had found satisfaction by bringing both the physical and the intellectual into obedience to the spiritual force of life. Relationship with God, as they knew him to be in Christ, was the most important focus of their lives.

There is an inner compulsion in such people, whether they are young college students or adults in productive life or mature citizens in retirement: they can't keep their faith to themselves. They all readily identify with the testimony of the great missionary E. Stanley Jones, who said repeatedly, "The moment I had repented of my sins and knew that God had forgiven me for Christ's sake, I felt so loved that I wanted in turn to love the whole world to Jesus."

College age believers, with their memory still fresh with the joy and zeal of their personal commitment to Christ, are often more persistent and more pervasive than those who have "matured in their faith". For such young people, the "must" of being born again is not optional! Much in the same way as football fans pump themselves up at pep rallies, Christians on university campuses similarly meet in groups— large and small—to encourage and challenge one another. In prayer they find both guidance and power for their lives. They learn an intimate leadership from God, plot their purpose and strategies, and set their goals.

By choice Ron Brown had wanted to have a high profile at Brown University, practically claiming it for his own. It was inevitable therefore, in the course of time, that he should sooner or later become an object of prayer and concern for those who care about the souls of other men and women. After all, why would any hunter go around poking at the bushes to try to scare up a rabbit if a gallant stag were prancing around the meadow in plain view just aching for attention. The would be football hero had set his goal on establishing a flashy image for himself. While still a freshman he attained a wide reputation. There was no mistaking who he was. He was a natural target for someone with evangelistic fervor.

Ron was sped through his freshman year by forces beyond his control. Quite instantly it was gone. He hardly had time to enjoy it. The coaches wanted his body and brain to build into a bruising defensive back. Their demands were constant. He gave his all to their prescribed program.

The professors wanted his mind to mold into a mental marvel. He loved the academic challenge. He applied himself studiously.

Ron didn't pause to judge the motives of the young ladies. He thrilled in the notoriety and thirsted for more.

His days were consumed by the heady swirl of those three contending, and often conflicting, forces. He laughed and joked openly in obvious enjoyment. Yet, in none of them did he find satisfaction. He yearned for something which would give a sense of lasting fulfillment. But what? He was haunted with a sense of emptiness—sometimes even while still standing in the limelight.

Fortunately there was yet another claim on his life. There was someone else, far more significant than all the others combined, who wanted him unselfishly. God had an eye on the boy whose bright face could so easily burst into a smile, whose dull heart bled with unrealized desires. God insightfully saw beyond the happy exterior to the sad interior wracked by uncertainty. God wanted Ron Brown's heart, mind, body, and soul. Not as a trophy. Not as a highly placed "Christian" athlete. God loved the young man. He wanted to be able to release him into the full measure of the purpose for which he was born, for which he was spared from a fetal death. God had a scope of life planned which was far beyond anything young Mr. Brown had ever hoped or imagined.

Ron thought he had raised up a new image of himself so as to take hold of everything he had been missing in life. Quite to the contrary, God had given him free reign knowing that such a prize would attract the best of his hunters. He was a marked man—by the grace of God.

One Tuesday night a group of campus Christians were studying the Bible together and sharing mutual concerns. One of the men named Vance spoke up, "You know, that freshman football player, Ron Brown?"

"Yeah, a star of the future," one pigskin enthusiast responded.

"He lives in my dormitory," Vance informed the group, "and I've been asking God to give me a chance to witness to him."

"Hey, man," another said, "just go up to the dude and nail him."

"Sure," Vance countered, "who do you think I am?

Brown's a big stick on campus! And I'm a nobody."

"Introduce yourself," a girl encouraged. "As far as we know, you've got something—someone—he doesn't. And he needs to hear it."

Vance took their advice, encouraged by their promises to pray for him. For two days he tried to build up the courage just to go to the man's room, knock on the door, walk in and introduce himself, tell him about Jesus and convert him. But he was afraid of rejection. He almost decided to give up on the whole idea. On the third day, however, as he rounded a corner of the dormitory building there was his target—all alone—in plain view—walking directly toward him.

Wow! Brown looked bigger and more fearsome than Vance had imagined in his prayer time.

Boldly, nonetheless, with an inner resource not his own, the timid Christian stepped into the middle of the sidewalk, extended his hand and introduced himself, "Hi, Ron. My name is Vance Watkins. I live in your dorm and just wanted to get to know you."

"Hey, man, how's it goin'?" Ron responded with his normal ready acceptance of others as he flashed his welcoming smile. "Yeah, I've seen you around a couple of times. It's good to meet you, Vance."

"Ron, I have an important question to ask you," the seemingly nobody blurted out while he had his momentum of courage, "Do you love the Lord?"

The simple question floored the macho athlete. He glanced around to see if anyone was looking. Had anyone else heard the question? Ron wished momentarily that he could roll up a corner of the sidewalk, crawl under it, and hide. He was totally, terribly embarrassed. He felt ill at ease. Although he had gone to church every Sunday of his life back home, he had never heard such a question. It was both confrontational and arrogant. How did any human being have the right to quiz another person in such a personal way? Yet, strangely, Ron was not offended. Rather than being repulsed by the thrust, his heart was pierced by an understanding of love he had never before encountered.

It seemed as if an eternity passed in the brief pause before he found the words to assure his new acquaintance, "Yeah, sure I love the Lord." Ron mouthed the words. He was at once sorry for that. He knew he had been asked an all important question and he had responded out of shock rather than from reason. He felt uncomfortable. He detested the all too familiar sense of inadequacy which arose within him. But at least he had successfully repelled the attack. He had given the man the response that he assumed was wanted. So he wouldn't be bothered again.

"Praise God!" Vance followed with surprise: he hadn't expected an instant success in his quest. "Tell me, Ron, how did you come to know the Lord?"

"What are you talkin' about, man?" Ron asked, confused. Hadn't he given the right answer? "No one 'knows' the Lord. He's not around here anywhere. How can you 'know the Lord'?"

"Why, you repent of your sins and ask Jesus to come into your heart," Vance answered simply, matter—of—factly. He didn't employ fancy psychology or salesmanship, but at least his theology was to the point.

Ron was impressed by the man's straightforwardness, but he was not pleased that he was the object of the unexpected attack. He wanted the conversation to end at once. "Hey," he responded with mounting anger in his voice, "I've been to church all my life. I've earned my stripes. I'm a pretty good guy. I don't need any more of this 'God' stuff."

Without worrying about tainting his image, Ron brushed passed the stalwart witness for Christ and ducked quickly into the dormitory. Vance was instantly shut out of his sight. But never again out of his mind. Never would he be able to forget the potent words that had come from the young man's lips. For that moment though, Ron was absorbed with anger. He tried not to appreciate the boldness of the young man. "Why did he come on so strong?" Ron wondered to himself. "Yeah, I'm going off a bit wild on this new image kick; and I know I probably shouldn't do that. But I'm cool with most people.

"I know one thing for sure: from now on I'm going to steer clear of people like Vance! I believe in God—and that's enough."

But that was not enough for God. The Lord who had created him desired an intimate relationship with the young man who had much to offer, the athlete who was looking only for personal gain, the seeker of a worldly success which would always elude him. God had plans for Ron Brown and was not about to quit just because he turned a cold shoulder to the first true witness who had been sent his way.

Ron thought he had ended the war and won the match by effecting his hasty retreat. That was far from accurate. It was not even the end of the first inning, and there was no score. The bell had not sounded yet for round two, and he was behind on points. The hounds were loose and running, and the prey was yet in sight. The game was still in the first quarter, and the ball was in God's hands. Only the first shot had been fired. The battle was set. And God was not about to quit.

Though Vance never approached him again to talk about Jesus, it seemed to Ron that he encountered a "Vance" at every juncture of the campus. Surely that was an exaggerated feeling. But it was evidenced by the fact that in the ensuing months he ran into several others who called themselves Christian. It seemed to Ron that he was beset by a band of men and women who were constantly talking about God. Those who lived closest to his room in the dorm, next door and down the hall, were Christians. Bold Christians! His head seemed to throb with the repeated inquiries:"Ron, do you love the Lord? Are you saved? Are you a Christian?"

He was becoming gun shy. It seemed he was the object of continual target practice.

One thing he had to admit in their favor, though. Their questions were never taunting or demeaning. There was always a sense of sincerity in their approaches.

Notwithstanding, he held them at bay and began lamely to retaliate. He refused to discuss with any of them the idea of a personal relationship with God. That was his defensive strategy. He knew that he had no knowledge with which to combat them. At first he tried simply to avoid them, but they turned up at the most inopportune, unexpected times and places. So he teamed up with his buddies, who were not Christian, to ridicule those they tagged as the "God Squad". They hung out together, doggedly taunting the believers when they came by.

Ron thought that would be a fatal blow to those whom he considered spiritual fanatics.

Spending the summer back home after his freshman year was a welcome release from college stress. Being again in the familiar surroundings, which he long had considered so restrictive, was a soothing balm to his soul. He obediently played church with his family and friends. In so doing he was strangely reaffirmed in his confused conviction that the term "Christian" was a title that people who were too religious assumed for themselves.

But soon the weeks seemed to slow down to a snail's pace. Ron wanted back into the university swing. He was increasingly anxious to return to Providence, glad he could hit the campus early for the August football practices, back to the fast track, into the full swing of freedom from the home ties.

His first year performance at Brown had attracted the approving attention of the coaching staff. There was no holding him back as a sophomore. The resulting new status as an acclaimed starter on defense for the varsity set him in even higher profile on campus. He wanted to savor every minute, to bask in the midst of the hype and glory. But he couldn't completely enjoy it. He was smart enough to know that in the glare of that limelight he was a constant mark for Campus Crusade people and other evangelical witnesses. They simply would not go away. He was amazed that they knew no fear. It actually seemed that the more he and his friends made fun of them the more persistent they became.

But he held his ground. They would not get him.

One startling event did get his attention, however. As he headed off for class one morning, the whole dormitory, the whole campus was abuzz with the tragic news that a fellow student athlete, Howard Lewis (an excellent cross country runner), had died in his sleep. The seemingly healthy young man had turned out the lights, gone to bed; but never got up again. He had choked in his sleep and had drowned in his own vomit. It was a sudden shock and sweeping sadness blanketed even those who didn't know him. The certain uncertainty of death had struck very close at hand.

Ron sat down at lunch that day with Rachelle James, whom he had dated frequently. After a short greeting, their meeting slid into silence. Without confronting the tragedy there was not much to talk about. But Ron didn't want to discuss death and idle chatter seemed out of place at such a time.

Rachelle, however, shortly broke through the impasse. There was one primary thought in her head and she had to get it said. "You know, Ron," she spoke in a thoughtful drawl, "Howard was absolutely healthy. I can't get over that. There was absolutely nothing wrong with him."

She paused in her contemplation. "He was so alive and healthy just yesterday!"

Again she marveled silently before concluding, "You just don't know when you're going to die, do you?"

Ron made no response. He pretended to be concentrating on his food. Truth of the matter was he was doing his best to ignore the lurking enemy of death. He didn't even want to give voice to the possibility, edged in fact, that someday death would come knocking on his door.

Yes! He knew Howard Lewis was healthy!

Yes! He himself was an excellent specimen of healthy manhood!

No! He did not know when he was going to die!

No! He was not going to think about it!

Chapter 6
HEY MAN!
YOU'RE GREAT!

• •

Summertime, 1977, once again was a welcome rest for Ron Brown at the conclusion of his sophomore year. It had been a grueling, tough, unbelievably frustrating year. On the one hand he had gloried in the steady acclaim as a rising star athlete in the Ivy League. But the grandeur was tempered by a realization that most of those friendships were extremely shallow and meaningless. This was boldly underscored as he battled a seemingly constant barrage of persistent Christian witness. Sports fans only sought him when he was hot. The Bible thumpers were after him continually.

He knew there was a significant difference. He could have savored the adoration and ignored the God Squad if it had not been for a gnawing doubt of insufficiency in his inner person. His desire for recognition was unending. But he masked it. By all means possible he sought to hide his own sense of inferiority which had plagued his every step from early childhood. He doubted himself and he knew it.

For the last several weeks of the spring term he had looked forward to summer, wanting to distance himself from the extreme competition for top dog status. He needed a break from the pressures of being sought after and being wanted just for the benefit of other people's pleasure.

The hoped-for-relief from stress promised to be better than ever before because he was headed for new surroundings. He was to be in Los Angeles with Mike, one of his Brown University Bruin teammates. Within a week of his arrival in California he shifted thankfully into the comfort zone of minimal demands and boundless relaxation. Then, however, he and Mike received similar letters from a group of those persistently concerned Christians back at the University.

"Am I safe nowhere?" He wondered. "How did they track me down, way out here?

Dear Ronny:

We hope you are having a great summer away from the books and enjoying new sights and experiences.

We also wanted to encourage you that you're not forgotten here at good ole Brown University. During this summer term there are not many of us around and the pace is a lot slower. But that gives us more time to get together for fellowship, so our prayer and Bible study group meets five mornings a week to keep things going.

We want you to know that we pray for you regularly. We trust God to save your soul so that you can begin to apply all your great potential for the good of Christ's Kingdom.

Romans 3:23 says that, 'All have sinned and fallen short of the glory of God.' That includes you and us.

Because of our sins, Romans 6:23 declares that 'The wages of sin is death, but the gift of God is eternal life through our Lord Jesus Christ.'

That gift of eternal life is God's provision for us all, as Jesus says in John 3:16, 'For God so loved the world that he gave his one and only son so that whoever believes in him shall not perish but have eternal life.' You can personalize that thought by inserting your own name — 'If Ron Brown believes in Jesus he shall not perish but have eternal life.'

All God asks of us is that we change our way and turn to him. I John 1:9 promises, 'If we confess our sins, he is faithful and just and will forgive us our sins and purify us from all unrighteousness.'

We here at Brown are sincerely praying that you will open your heart to Jesus Christ even now.

We look forward to having you back on campus in August. In the meantime if we can do anything for you please let us know.

Love in Christ,

Ron was not pleased as he read the message. Indeed, he was greatly angered and offended. The Bible totin' crew at the university had gone too far. The two athletes agreed that the letter was all the more proof that the whole bunch were wild-eyed fanatics and were not to be taken seriously.

"How dare they intrude into my private life like this," Ron declared resentfully. "Just when I thought I was free from their nagging they have to send a screwy letter about Jesus and sin and all that stuff."

"Awh, forget it," advised his friend, who wasn't so sensitive to religious issues and therefore not so easily pricked. "They're just a bunch of losers who need somebody to judge so that they won't feel so worthless."

However, Ron was not easily turned from his wrath. His anger burned hot. "Will they ever be sorry they wrote this letter. I will make their lives miserable when I get back to Providence," he vowed.

But his vow of revenge was idly made. He didn't have it within himself to willfully harm anyone. What he truly intended, or wanted, was just to be able to successfully avoid the whole lot of them.

The remaining days of vacation passed all too quickly and Ron returned to Brown for the preseason practice sessions. In those intervening weeks he had religiously, purposefully excluded all thought of Jesus Christ and his campus champions from his conscious mind. His attention was focused entirely on using the weeks of training to sharpen his skills which had earned him a starting position the previous season and which had extended his football notoriety beyond the campus.

Having kept active with physical activity while on the West Coast, his body quickly adjusted to the rigorous demands of the training regimen. He was anxious for the first day with pads—and contact scrimmaging.

He was totally absorbed in football. Between the hours of physical training and the brain draining sessions of learning the details of the playbook, Ron gave little thought to God or the barrage of witnesses which had come his way the previous year. He had even forgotten about the summer letter until late one night after he'd gone to bed. Unable to go to sleep it suddenly dawned on him that he'd been back in Providence for ten full days and no one had bothered him about his need of being "saved".

"Perhaps they finally got smart and gave up," he smiled sadly to himself.

Just as quickly, however, his smile turned upside down with an unexplainable fear that perhaps indeed they had given up on him. He did not sleep well that night.

Camaraderie began to build as composition of the team took form around the returning lettermen. Ron and the other veteran players took stock of the new batch of sophomores who served mostly as live practice targets. Harry Walls was one such player. He shared the locker next to Ron's. The two of them had not met the previous year, for the simple reason that varsity jocks just don't spend much time watching freshmen play. Besides, as a first year player Harry had made no noteworthy contribution even to the freshman team. He had no special athletic ability to draw attention to himself. To Ron, the man seemed much too timid to be a gutsy football player. Yet at the same time, Harry had a strength in his gentleness which was strangely attractive.

It was into the second week of practice before Ron and Harry finally had an occasion for more than a passing moment of greeting. They were just leaving the locker room when both stopped for a drink at the water fountain.

"Hey, Ron, you had a great practice today," Harry said enthusiastically.

"Thanks," Ron responded, wondering to himself. "What's this guy trying to say." Certainly it wasn't unusual for someone to compliment him on having played an outstanding game. But never had another player made such a comment after a day of mere gut grinding drills.

"I love the way you really put yourself into it," Harry continued, as they walked up the ramp out of the fieldhouse. "It's just the way God made us," he added unapologetically, "you know, like it says in 1 Corinthians 10:31, '...Whatever you do, do it all for the glory of God.'"

Ron gaped at the man, speechless. Wasn't it enough that he'd have to try to get away from the fanatics in the dormitory and across the campus! Now he finds that one of these jokers had a football locker right next to his. He was about to tell the man to get lost before being confronted with the inevitable question, "Ron, do you love the Lord?"

But before he could speak a negative word, Harry broke off the conversation, "Well, Ron, I've got to run. I'll see you in the morning at practice."

Ron was astounded as the lanky athlete turned and headed on his way. This was the first time he'd heard someone talk personally about God without being pushy. He no longer felt defensive. He dropped his guard as he watched the man go. Walking to his dorm Ron could not help but ask himself, "How do you do something for the glory of God?"

Ron never got around to asking Harry the question. He didn't have to. He got an answer without even being aware of it.

Harry was one of those rare types of men who seemed to be able to handle everything in stride, no matter how difficult. Similar circumstances could possibly turn another individual inside out. But not Harry. The man seemed to have a smile painted on his slender face. At least by all outward appearance, he was always happy.

Notwithstanding, Ron kept a wary eye on the man. He had become gun shy from the persistency of other "Bible toters" on campus and he was certain that Harry would pounce on him sooner or later. As he watched—always at arms length—he was more and more confused by what he saw. He thought the man definitely was weird. Try as he may, he could not understand Harry's attitude. Ron's primary definition of success at that juncture of his life was to be a starter on the football team. More than that to be a truly good player, a standout, a star. He sought recognition. He sought popularity and its immediate gratification of status with the girls and the guys. Harry's manner, on the other hand, was in stark contrast to Ron's best laid plans through his two full years at Brown University. Could Harry have a potent secret behind his cool demeanor? The thought began to gnaw away at Ron that perhaps there was something wrong with his own concept of success.

In the team's season opener against Yale Ron played a spectacular game overall. But he blew a key assignment which led to Yale's only touchdown which was, in turn, enough for their margin of victory. The Bruins wound up losing 10-9; which put them out of the driver's seat for the Ivy League championship.

The Brown locker room was a sullen place. No glad back slapping and high fives and congratulations. Ron soaked a long time in a hot shower. He was wound tight. In his mind he replayed the second quarter of the game over and over. But no matter how he tried to redo it; every time he failed. He missed the play. He blew it. It was a long, quiet ride back to Providence on the team bus.

Ron somehow survived a morbid weekend. No one had openly blamed him for the loss, but he was certain they must. He dreaded facing the team at practice on Monday. As soon as he stepped onto the field, however, Harry came running up to him with praise on his lips. He spoke vividly of everything right Ron had done in Saturday's game. There was no mention of the one mistake.

"Was this guy talking about the same game?" Ron wondered to himself. Since Harry was not on the traveling squad, perhaps he had missed some pertinent details in the radio account.

Ron, nonetheless, accepted the praise, without complaint. He really needed the boost; and there was no doubting the warmth and obvious sincerity by which Harry spoke. It only bothered Ron that he was not able to return the compliment. There was nothing, in all honesty, for which he could applaud Harry, he thought, at least in regards to football prowess.

Ron was still thinking about Harry after practice as he stood a long time in the hot spray of the shower. Finally he stepped out of the shower, dried himself, and weaved his way around equipment and benches, slowly back to his locker. "Now, look at this guy," he thought to himself, as he studied Harry out of the corner of his eye, "he doesn't even get into the game. He doesn't play a down. He's a bench warmer. He doesn't even play much in practice. Yet he's always smiling. Always happy."

Ron shook his head in disbelief and started to dress, still deep in his own thoughts. "This guy is out of touch with reality. He just doesn't understand what is important in life. He's not pushing himself. He's not doing all he can. Yet, he's still happy.

"I just don't get it."

But Harry was applying himself and doing all he could. However, unlike Ron, his definition of success was based on process rather than results.

Harry had already dressed. He shut his locker and turned toward Ron with his hand extended for a final congratulatory shake. "I just want to tell you again what a great game you played on Saturday."

"Thanks," Ron said lamely.

With that, Harry walked away, leaving Ron more confused than ever.

The entire season progressed that way. Ron playing. Harry watching. Ron fearing a spiritual onslaught. Harry offering endless praise. It didn't matter to Harry whether it was practice or competition, his remarks of admiration were consistent and constant:

"Hey, man you made a great play on that last down in practice.

"That was a fantastic tackle on Jones.

"You must have leaped four feet on that interception.

"I love the way you run.

"I love the way you play."

Not one time did he express displeasure or resentment at not playing himself. His words of praise were always honest and tactically correct. Often he weaved a quote from the Bible into what he said, but never did he twist his words as a weapon against the more superior athlete.

Ron thought the guy was a little strange. Even so, he liked him and had an unspoken admiration for his zeal.

Late in the season, after a grueling, hard fought win over Harvard, Ron and his buddies celebrated late into the night. It was no fun getting up Sunday morning. He groaned as he rolled out of bed. It was after eleven o'clock when he strolled into the cafeteria to wait for the lunch line to open. He slouched in a chair, dressed in faded jeans and a sloppy sweatshirt. With a ball cap on backward, he was acting the clown for the entertainment of his friends.

In walked Harry. Fresh from church. He looked handsome in a suit and tie. A Bible was grasped in his right hand.

As Harry approached the cluster of men, men who were supposedly his football teammates, they began a chorus of taunts:

"Hey, man, check out Harry!"

"Yeah, Harry the home boy."

"Don't he look cute with his Bible and suit."

Harry made no reply. He kept his focus straight ahead.

He smiled thinly as he walked on by. Without comment he took a place, all alone, in the growing line at the serving table. The insults faded into nothingness. The man's true bearing increased right before Ron's eyes.

As he watched Harry pass by, a sudden, intense sense of admiration for him swept over Ron. He whispered to himself, "Boy! You know there's something about this guy! Man, I respect him. It's not just the compliments he gives me, but there's something deep about this guy. I'm being tossed and turned like a leaf in the wind by my friends. Others are dictating my life by my sensitivity to what they say. They're making the moves in life—actually we're doing it to each other. Like puppets.

"But here's a guy who walks his own path. Here's a guy who doesn't care what other people think or say."

Of course, Ron didn't dare let his buddies know what he was really thinking. He only looked at them and chimed in, "Yeah, there's something about that guy."

"Someday," Ron affirmed to himself, "I'm going to tell Harry how much I appreciate him as a man."

Chapter 7
GOD'S ULTIMATE
WEAPON

● ●

His junior year with the Brown University Bruins was a triumph for Ron Brown. The Ivy League football coaches and New England sportswriters had an opinion of him almost equal to that of the ever-praising Harry Walls. He was an unanimous selection to First Team All Ivy League. That, in turn, spurred his thinking and inflamed his vision beyond college to a professional career. Wasting little time, scouts from various pro teams began sending letters to him regarding their interest. They sought details to begin formulating their draft plans for the future. Without complaint he was caught up in an ego-boosting whirlwind.

But the hype of athletic achievement is fleeting. With the end of the first semester, the glory of victories and the despair of failures during the football season faded into history. Ron had time finally to give himself to the pursuit of another interest.

He had first seen her in September as he and his buddies checked out the more than 100 newcomers at the Minority Students Orientation. On that first occasion she had smiled in recognition of his presence, and he had nodded in noble response. From that brief exposure she had been indelibly etched into his mind.

He chided himself twice during the fall when he saw her on campus, "Man, get your act together. Just trot across the grass. Walk up, put on the charm, smile, and ask her out."

But each time, all too quickly, as he hesitated to build up his nerve, the opportunity vanished and he'd kick himself.

It was not until February that he, who was so brazen on the gridiron, overcame his timidity and fear of rejection to boldly ask her for a date.

Normally he had no real apprehension in approaching anyone. Though internally insecure, he had an outrageous compulsion to at least act with confidence. In this case, however, he also was unsure of whether or not he even wanted to commit himself. When he saw her he also perceived a warning not to get involved. For he had inquired about her from others and learned that she was one of those "Jesus fanatics". That was enough to give him serious doubts as to whether or not anything worthwhile could come from such a relationship. Nonetheless, there was something so appealing about her that he decided that since he had been able to withstand the pressures to "convert" from all the other Bible thumpers that he could surely stand up against a single, slender young woman.

Not only was Audrey Dixon lovely to look at; she had quality on the inside as well. She was certain of what was important in life and why. She had solid goals set and was determined to reach them. None of that, however, had come her way with ease.

Audrey had been rescued from being a shameful product of one of the worst slums of the inner city of New York. Her mother had to double as a father since that man had not stayed around to shoulder any responsibility for Audrey, her sister, or her brother. In spite of the daily threatening push of drug dealers, constant reminders of violence and insecurity from the street gangs, Audrey's mother succeeded in keeping at least one of her daughter's safe from irreparable turmoil. She stayed in school, made good grades, and gained recognition at prestigious Stuyvesant High School.

At that point, one of the truly significant minority assistance programs, "A Better Chance", stepped in to offer Audrey a scholarship to attend Philip Exeter Boarding School.

By sheer grit and determination, she had done well at Stuyvesant. But under the gentler atmosphere at Exeter, Audrey gracefully flowered into full bloom. Her keen mind propelled her through her studies successfully, until, as a graduating senior she was honored as salutatorian of the class. Just as importantly and significantly, however, at Exeter she was confronted with the Gospel of Jesus Christ and turned control of her life into his hands.

For their first date, Ron decided on the safety of a movie for in such a situation a guy doesn't have to expend his efforts on detailed conversation in order to become intimate with a girl. Was he in for a surprise! Audrey was not impressed at being in the presence of a campus football star. If her date for the evening had been the "least likely to succeed" of the entire student body, her primary goal still would have been to get into serious communication.

Little wonder then that they did not make it to the theater that night. She was right on time when he called for her at the dormitory. It was easy for him to find something to say from the start, "Hey, you look nice!" Because that was the obvious truth. Beyond that, however, he had been searching desperately all the way to her dorm for a line to follow.

But not to worry. Audrey had an agenda. She had heard a lot *about* Ron Brown. Her goal for the evening was to get to know who he really was.

"Thank you," she responded as he helped her on with her coat. "You look nice yourself, Sir."

Ron felt a surge of importance within as she firmly locked her arm in his as they stepped out the door, into the brisk winter night. That simple gesture from her signaled an unspoken expression of, "Please protect me!" And his instant reaction was positive. He would do just that.

They began to talk as they walked; and shortly they both were so caught up in conversation that by common consent they stopped in a coffee shop. Three hours later, having ignored going to the movie, Ron walked her home. He was fascinated with the girl as he left her dormitory. Never had he opened up to any other person so freely.

Courting Audrey was a challenge for Ron like no other he had ever confronted. It was obvious from their first date that she was open to building a relationship with him: but not at just any price. In spite of the harsh background from which she came, her commitment to Jesus Christ two years earlier had revolutionized her life. She was a Christian with definite parameters. She knew who knew what was best for her and she was determined not to stray from His plan for her life. If the budding friendship with Ron Brown was to be a significant part of that plan—fine. If not—that too would be fine.

Audrey was especially interesting to Ron because she was a multi-dimensional person. He had gained the impression from the first zealous witnesses for Christ on campus that they had only one goal in life—his heart for Jesus. Harry had altered his view somewhat, but Audrey was like a first chapter in a new book. She introduced him to a new concept of friendship, openness, and vitality which excited him about the prospect of getting beyond mere introductions. However, that was no easy task. She was not a pushover for a varsity leather jacket. And even as a freshman her time was consumed with the demands of countless friends, an intense program of study set toward a doctorate in psychology, and a loyalty to regular attendance at the "Romans 8:28 Bible Study" on campus.

"Ron, I truly did enjoy our time together the other night," Audrey said with a lilt in her voice as they walked across campus together a few days later. "And I don't want to push my convictions on you. But you can't expect me to fit my schedule to suit yours. You know that Jesus Christ is the most important part of my life and I spend a lot of time developing my relationship with him through Bible study and prayer groups."

"I don't understand that much about religion, but I do know I want to..." Before he could finish his sentence, their conversation was interrupted by another couple who anxiously called Audrey over to them in front of the library.

"Please excuse me for a second, Ron, I'll be right back," she said assuredly.

Ron did not follow her, but watched with resentment burning inside his chest. He was incensed. He knew what was up—and he was specifically excluded. The young man was a self-proclaimed leader of the "God Squad". He had attacked Ron with the Bible several times, but had never been able to break through his outer defenses.

"Audrey," the young man declared loudly enough for Ron to overhear, "that guy is not a good influence on you. He's not a believer. In fact, he's an outspoken critic of everything we do. He'll pull you down with him."

The young woman who was with them looked at Ron cautiously out of the corner of her eyes, as if she were peeking at the devil himself.

Ron complied with a sly smirk. The young woman anxiously turned her attention back to the teaching of the college guru.

"Listen," Audrey said without apology. "I like him. He's fun to be with."

"Don't get sucked in by all that charm and athletic mystique. We're not supposed to compromise our faith in Christ."

"I'm not compromising my faith," Audrey answered with a growing irritation evident in the tone of her voice.

"Well, did you tell him about Jesus and that he needs to be born again?," the woman demanded piously.

"Yeah!" Her companion rejoined emphatically.

"He knows where I stand," Audrey responded flatly. "But beyond that it's none of your business what Ron and I talk about."

"Oh, Audrey, 'Do not take lightly the instruction of a brother,'" the young lady coined a proverb.

"Yes, listen to the advice of Saint Paul," the young man said solemnly, "'Do not be yoked together with nonbelievers.'"

"We're certainly not 'yoked'," Audrey assured them with a soft, secretive voice as she turned to go. "But you certainly have heightened my interest. Perhaps God intends to use me for Ron's benefit."

Undoubtedly God would use her. But how? In what way? The athlete intended to pursue a relationship with the lovely young woman from New York. But he was equally intent on avoiding the religious functions that consumed so much of her time. He had plenty to content himself with as he filled in those gaps. In no way was he interested in opening himself up to an interrogation on the status of his soul by others of the crusaders for Christ.

The understanding between the two of them broadened and deepened. They enjoyed being friends. Ron was thankful to have someone he could confide in without the fear of rebuke or rejection. She gave him a sense of confidence. Audrey assured him that it was all right just to be. To be who he truly was and not merely the happy-go-lucky clown he tried so hard to project. For her part, Audrey also gained from the friendship. Though Ron could not share with her spiritually, what was of greatest significance to her, she knew that he respected her as a person, as someone of worth. And coming from a nonbeliever she considered that to be quite a compliment. She frequently invited him to the many and varied special occasions of the Christian community, but Ron was not very responsive. He ducked into church with her twice, just because there had been too long a hiatus without seeing her. However, he fended off her gentle reminders that her primary goal in life was what should concern him as well: to perfect the purpose for which God brought us into life.

As the school year came to a close, Ron was not as keen as in previous years to get off campus and get home. He had learned to appreciate Audrey more than any female friend he had known. He began to miss her even before leaving campus. He wished there were an "understanding" between them, one that would insure their relationship for the summer.

However, she had made it clear that they were just good friends.

After two weeks of slow summer fun, Ron could stand the separation no longer. He missed her terribly. He dialed her number in New York City. At the sound of her voice on the other end of the line his face brightened.

"Hey! How're-ya-doin'? This is Ron Brown."

She laughed at the formality of identifying himself. His insecurity was showing. "Yes, Ron! I'd recognize that baritone voice anywhere. It's so good to hear from you. What are you doing?"

"Oh, I'm playin' a lot of B-ball and trying to keep up with the social life my mom has for me. Since I got home she's had a constant parade of family and friends through the house."

Ron paused, wet his lips. His heart was thumping with a nervousness he'd never before experienced.

"Audrey!" He continued with determination. "I didn't call to talk about me. I just had to hear your voice. I miss you! I miss our walks and our talks."

"I miss you too," she responded honestly.

The creased furrows of anxiety faded from his brow. An unfamiliar and unfathomable joy swept through him. He couldn't recall ever having been "missed" by anyone before.

"I sure wish I could see you today," Ron moaned. "September seems so far away—almost forever."

"I'll write you a long letter this afternoon," she promised in consolation. "And I'll write you often."

"I'm not so good at writing," Ron confessed, "but I've got your number and I'll be calling again—and again—and again."

She laughed.

He loved her laugh.

Was the pagan athlete, entrenched, unmoved, immovable by the barrage of persistent witnesses on campus, unknowingly caught in a tender trap of unadorned Christian love? Not by a long shot. He of course knew she was a Christian, a very dedicated believer. But his feelings for her had nothing to do with Jesus. This was between man and woman. Audrey and Ron. He gave no thought to Jesus Christ as being in the picture at all.

Chapter 8
WHATEVER HAPPENED TO HARRY?
● ●

Audrey, who never committed herself to anything lightly, held true to her promise, she wrote often during that summer. Of everything she mailed, however, her second letter was Ron's favorite. He read and re-read it almost daily.

My Dear Ronny,

I just returned from a quiet, wonderful time alone at Battery Park. To be by oneself in New York City is quite a feat with people, people everywhere. But I've found that it's not necessary to lock out the sounds and combustion of the day in order to be truly alone. In fact, I experience a beautiful assurance of peace as I observe all that is going on around me while at the same time, looking inward to all that God is accomplishing in my life. In moments like these I sense that I am alone in the presence of the Lord and that he has set aside all his other activities just to take notice of me.

As I sat on a wooden park bench, with the sun warm on my face, the Statue of Liberty standing majestic in the distance, and with the incessant blare of the tug boat horns beating on my ears; I thought of you.

I laughed at myself as I imagined you standing as tall and assured as Miss Liberty. In a way you are alike —immovable; and I like that about you. You, as she, offer hope to others with your determination to achieve, to succeed.

So, I prayed for you in a special way as I sat there. I thought of all the amazing potential God has wrapped up in your mind, body, and soul. I made no plea. I simply again entrusted you to his care. I'm confident that he will in his time enable you to accomplish all his purpose for your being.

Of course, one of those purposes is already being perfected. For the very thought of you brings joy into my life.

With love,

Audrey

Ron also kept his promise. He called often. Between those moments of special, but all too brief, communication the summer passed with speed.

In addition to stoking the fires of love, however, Ron also had his days filled with his own hectic and rigorous patterning of physical training. He intended to arrive at the preseason training camp with the Bruins in the best possible condition. He had a shot at being a high draft choice by the pros and he intended to succeed beyond all measure in his senior season. Eyes, the important eyes of scouts, would be searching the stadiums of America every Saturday. He was determined that they would take notice of what he intended to be the most outstanding defensive back in the Ivy League and one of the best in America.

Heading back to Providence the second week of August, with Audrey not due to return from New York until after the first of September, Ron's thoughts of friendship centered on the other Christian he respected, Harry Walls. He had not seen the tall, lanky athlete much during the spring semester; but when he did the man always had a word of encouragement for him. He was looking forward to seeing the guy again. Especially, he began planning in his mind how he would tell Harry that he truly did appreciate him and valued his friendship. He wasn't very good at putting together "corny" words; but he wanted somehow to apologize. He sensed an urgency to erase from his memory the guilt of having stood silently by while others ridiculed the "Bible toter".

Ron enjoyed rappin' with other players that first night back in the dorm; but Harry wasn't there. Brown was not an inexpensive school, so Harry lived off campus in order to cut expenses. Ron realized, in the midst of the fun of the evening, that he wished Harry were present to put some meaning into the otherwise boring conversation. He began counting the hours to the warmup practice the next morning. He wanted to get on with the task of building a stronger relationship with the incomparable benchwarmer.

When Ron got to the locker room there were a lot of other old friends to greet that he had not seen the night before. He kept looking beyond the milling players to catch a glimpse of Harry. The man was nowhere in sight. At last the talking and joking subsided and Ron headed for his locker to change clothes. Only then did he realize that the locker next to his was empty. No sign of Harry.

Hurriedly he put on his sweatsuit and tennis shoes and went directly to the equipment manager. "Hey, John, where's Harry Walls? His locker's empty."

"Harry's not comin' back." John replied flatly.

"What do you mean, 'he's not comin' back'?" Ron demanded with a sense of urgency.

"Well, he decided to transfer to another school," John answered.

"I'm really sorry to hear he transferred," Ron said sadly. "Maybe he finally came to his senses. Perhaps he went to a school where he can have a chance to play football."

Ron turned away from the equipment room and headed to the field. A gloom overrode his spirit. Why had he not grasped the relationship with Harry when it was in reach. He felt an inexpressible loneliness, yet there was something about Harry which would never leave him. His respect for the man was deep, though he doubted he'd ever see him again or have the opportunity to tell him the impact he'd had on his life.

Notwithstanding, Ron did not lament the lost opportunity for long. There was too much to accomplish. He plunged with intensity into the football program. He had arrived for the season with spirited determination and pushed the memory of the fourth stringer out of conscious thought. He worked hard. He was ready from day one for the two-a-day sessions—even for pads on scrimmage. His own enthusiasm served to pump up the team morale to a fever pitch. Indeed! This last season of his collegiate career was going to be fantastic.

Then the schedule started. Perhaps it was due to the absence of Harry, with the man's constant and unsolicited compliments. Perhaps it was due to the pressure he put on himself to keep trying always to do even better, to break some of the standards he'd set as a junior. Perhaps it was the high expectations others expressed. Perhaps it was the inconsistency of the pro scouts: one day buddying up to him and another time ignoring him. Whatever it was, nothing he did on the football field satisfied Ron Brown.

It's a good thing Audrey arrived back on campus a few days early, ahead of the opening game of the season. Ron Brown, the brash, bold athlete, desperately needed someone to talk with, to confide in. To whom could he share his fears?

Audrey listened as Ron poured out his frustrations.

"You know," he said with a disbelieving shake of his head, "probably the worst thing that can happen to a college athlete is to have a really good junior year because then all of a sudden everybody has great expectations for your senior year.

"I just don't know what I can do more than I am doing now. I'm in top shape. I know the playbook both ways from Sunday. I give it my best effort. And nothin'! I feel nothin'! There's just no juice in it. Or somethin'."

"Ronny," Audrey suggested quietly, "I don't know a lot about football. In fact, I probably wouldn't go to a game except to watch you. But I do know that you're trying too hard. Let me read you something that just may give you a new slant on it.

"The Apostle Paul experienced many difficulties in his life and there was one problem he prayed and prayed about. It had him flustered. He loved and served God, but, he never got the answer he wanted."

Without apology she took a New Testament out of her purse, turned to 2 Corinthians 12:8-10 and read:

> Three times I pleaded with the Lord to take it away from me. But he said to me, "My grace is sufficient for you, for my power is made perfect in weakness." Therefore I will boast all the more gladly about my weaknesses, so that Christ's power may rest on me. That is why, for Christ's sake, I delight in weaknesses, in insults, in hardships, in persecutions, in difficulties. For when I am weak, then I am strong.

"Wow! That's heavy stuff," Ron observed. "What was the guy's problem?"

"No one knows for sure," Audrey answered simply. "But this scripture has helped to assure me that the world doesn't rest on my shoulders. I don't have to be Miss Perfect for everyone. When I admit that I'm weak and can't handle something—and turn it over to the Lord—he always comes through."

Ron felt an unusual calm in listening to her words. She didn't make it sound like she was preaching at him. She was sharing what had meaning for her. He liked that.

Throughout the season he turned to Audrey frequently for consolation, and she was always there with a good word. Yet he could not escape the aloneness, the insecurity that gripped him inwardly.

He tried constantly to please his friends. While they

were around, the joking kept him pumped up. However, they weren't with him twenty-four hours a day. When they were gone, the "good times" went with them. But, even worse, eventually he had to try to go to sleep—alone.

In spite of the fact that his emotions performed erratic cartwheels in his soul, at least his relationship with Audrey blossomed. She encouraged him through the difficult times. Invariably, in such moments, she would open her Bible and read to him, in much the same way as young David sang Psalms to soothe the troubled spirit of King Saul. In time, he started going back to church on Sundays—not that he put much of himself into it—but it helped fill a void which he could not express.

Of course, no relationship could ever last if it were entirely one sided. Audrey also had many insecurities: she had gone through many life-warping experiences before Christ came into her life. She too received from Ron. Mutually they shared the incredible encouragement of entrusting their soul burdens with one another. In a deepening friendship Audrey and Ron wisely built on each other's strengths.

Amazingly, Ron continued to do well in his studies though his mind was consumed with a desire to be a pro football player. He was shackled by that singleness of purpose. It was his passion. His goal. His first thought in the morning. His last thought at night.

As the season rolled around to mid-year the Brown Bruins were having just a so-so season. One week up, the next week down. Holy Cross was to be the next game. The Crusaders were undefeated. They had beaten a couple of really good teams and were ranked number one in the New England area. It was a big game, a home game for the Bruins. ABC scheduled it for Eastern regional television coverage. A win would turn the entire season around for Brown University, but a loss would doom the team to a dismal season.

Going into the game the Bruins were rated heavy underdogs even though they were playing in their own stadium.

Of course, predicting is an inexact science. Any team can beat any other on a given day. Ron and his teammates arrived at the locker room shortly before noon, having read all the dismal forecasts concerning their fate for the day. As they geared up for the game they expressed their anger to each other at having been described so miserably by sportswriters—even in the local press. Slowly they began seething. As the coach entered into his pep talk their anger was kindled into flame. By game time they burst onto the field like a great ball of fire.

Holy Cross didn't even think to get the license number from the truck that smeared it across the turf. Early in the fourth quarter the scoreboard told an amazing story in bold block numbers - Brown 31 - Holy Cross 10. The coach decided at that point to get his starters out and let the substitutes finish the mopping up job.

As the regulars came out, to the thunderous roar of the partisan crowd, everyone was high-fiving one another and bouncing around hugging each other. Everyone on the Brown sideline felt joy, happiness and gladness. Everyone except Ron Brown.

He sat there on the brink of tears. He couldn't understand his own emotions. He had played one of the best, if not the very best game, of his career. He was to receive the game ball for his efforts. Yet all he could think about was the terrible pressure he was under at that particular moment. Pressure he was putting on himself because of the television coverage and the many pro scouts in the stands.

"How could I have missed that tackle in the first quarter," he bemoaned to himself. "If it weren't for me they wouldn't have even gotten their one touchdown.

"What in the world are the scouts thinking now?

"I bet they all left in disgust that they wasted their time coming clear up here to watch a nobody."

He sighed in despair as he thought of the ribbing he was sure to face in the dormitory, in the dining hall, on the campus. "I wonder if my friends saw my colossal error on that last play of the third quarter? No one will forget that for a long, long time."

In his panic Ron walked wearily to the end of the bench and sat down. Everybody else continued to celebrate as the game wound down.

Brad, one of his best friends on the team, came to where he sat and looked down at him in unbelief. "Hey, Brown! Man, you look like you just lost your dad or somethin'."

"I know," Ron replied sadly. "That's just the way I feel—and I don't understand it."

On the team bus, for the ride back to the locker room, after the victory was secured, the celebration continued. Everybody was jostling around, shouting and giving victory cheers. Ron just sat there in his own personal gloom, staring blankly out the window. He didn't dare look around at anyone. He didn't want to be seen. But he listened keenly, waiting for someone to declare, "Did you see that play Ron messed up back in the third quarter."

He was paranoid, sitting there with rabbit ears, waiting for taunting that never came. He was tight in mind and body. He wondered what Harry Walls would've said about this game. He was certain that even the ever optimistic Harry could not think of a compliment now. Ron went back to his dormitory room alone. He laid down on his bed in mental anguish. To break the spell he tried counting the ceiling tiles—over and over again. It didn't work.

"There's something terribly wrong," he admitted to himself. "Something just isn't right inside."

Brown University proceeded to win its next five games, only to lose to the David Shula-led Dartmouth Big Green for the Ivy League Championship. Nonetheless, the experts were saying that Ron had an outstanding season. Though the NFL draft was months away, not until the end of April, rumors and opinions were rampant. People who supposedly were in the know kept Ron in turmoil and under pressure with their unsolicited views.

First one would say, "You'll be drafted in the third

round."

That would make the young man giddy with excitement as the visions of a signing bonus and a six figure salary raced through his mind.

Another would express his opinion, "You're bound to make it in the sixth round, seventh for sure."

With such queer, erratic pressure Ron's mood swings were just as unpredictable. Besides his own discipline of sticking to his studies there were two other release valves for him. Two outlets which were strangely, diametrically opposites: the steadying influence of Audrey Dixon and the occasional carefree partying with his friends.

One such late night of carousing followed the senior fling at one of the Greek houses. Though Ron had never pledged to a fraternity, his status as an athlete made him a sought after guest for many functions.

He awoke the next morning with a brain breaking hangover. To boot, he was bummed out with himself, the football hassle, the study grind, and life in general. Though it was exam time, he decided to forget all responsibilities for the day and just slouch around. Somehow he hoped to recover from the anguish raging in his body which fluctuated between his churning stomach and throbbing head.

Audrey happened to encounter him in the student lounge. His body was contorted sideways in an overstuffed chair with his head propped uncomfortably on the armrest. She took one look at his rumpled appearance and knew there was big trouble. "Ron," she said calmly, hiding her annoyance at his irresponsible behavior, "what are you doing here? Don't you have a sociology exam at eleven?"

"I'm not goin'," he responded unevenly as he sat up in agony to face her. "I don't feel so good."

"You're drunk!" She scolded.

"Was drunk." He corrected, with a limp smile. "At the moment I'm merely miserable."

"Well, miserable or not," she demanded, "you've got to get to that class."

"But, I'm not prepared," he admitted.

"Then fake it!" She advised as she grabbed his right arm with both her hands to force him to his feet. "With your intelligence you'll make something out of it."

As he sat through the exam, preserving his grade point average, he took agonizing stock of himself. He came to three conclusions. One, he was an utter fool, because he had no clue who he was as a man. Two, he was thankful for Audrey Dixon, for she was a true friend who cared for him as a person. Three, he was going to be a pro football player because...because success was the only way he could prove himself worthy of life. Otherwise he was a loser. He just had to be drafted.

His self involvement and preoccupation with his own concerns was total. However, his concentration on himself was jarred a few weeks later when he got a call late one afternoon from Audrey's roommate. "Ron, Audrey needs you at the campus infirmary right away. There was an accident at the softball field and the doctor's examining her right now."

"What happened?" He insisted anxiously.

"She was standing on the sidelines at the softball game and was hit by a wild throw from second base. It really looks serious. She was hit right at the edge of her left eye. She could lose her vision."

"I'll be right there." Ron promised.

Ron, dodging others as if returning an interception for a touchdown, ran all the way to the clinic. The news of the accident spread rapidly across campus. By the time Ron arrived, breathless, a half-dozen other friends of the popular young lady from New York were already there. Uncertain as to what the prognosis would be they had huddled together in a corner of the lobby, hands linked together in a circle of prayer. Ron stood to one side, a solitary figure. He was thankful on the one hand that Audrey had so many concerned friends, but disgruntled on the other hand that he felt ill at ease. He didn't know how to join them in prayer.

When the doctor came out of the examining room fifteen

minutes later his opinion was guarded, and definitely not optimistic. "The swelling makes it impossible to check her vision thoroughly. Her eye suffered a terrific impact. The effects of the concussion will keep her in bed for at least a week."

He paused, then continued with a sigh, "There's a good chance she'll lose her vision."

Ron was devastated. "Why should anything so terrible happen to a person as kind and wonderful as Audrey?" He complained to himself.

"May we see her now?" Her roommate asked.

"Yes, but just for a few minutes—and only two of you at a time."

Ron stood to one side. Partly he wanted to be a gentleman and let others go first. More importantly he wanted to gather his thoughts so as to have something soothing to say when he saw her.

The room was quiet when he entered. All the others had gone. The sound of her breathing was exaggerated. With her nasal passages clogged, she sucked air in through her mouth.

Ron was not prepared for the gruesome sight as he stepped to the edge of her bed. The smooth lines of her angular face were grotesquely distorted by swelling, black and blue blotches cast an eerie glow to her bronzed skin.

"Hey, Audrey, how you doin'?" Ron asked. He was at a loss for words as he took her right hand in his.

"Fine," she lied bravely.

"I wish like anything, that this had happened to me instead of you." Ron declared as tears formed in his eyes.

"Well, if it had, you wouldn't be lying here," she replied. "You've been hit harder than this twenty times in a game—and you just bounce back."

"Yeah, but I have enough sense to wear a helmet," he joked.

She laughed lightly and began to cough.

"I'm sorry," he apologized, "I shouldn't be a clown at a time like this."

"No, no, that's all right," she assured him. "You're my favorite clown of all."

"Listen," he said, "I'd better get out of here so you can rest, but I'll be back tomorrow."

"Yes, I'm very tired," she agreed.

"Is there anything I can do for you?" He asked.

"Just pray for me," she advised.

"I sure will," he promised solemnly.

Throughout the night Ron fretted about his vow. He knew he loved her. How then could he have committed himself to an empty promise. He didn't know anything about praying. Nevertheless, he gave it his best shot. "God," he said unfamiliarly, "Audrey is one of yours. I'm not. So I just ask you to take care of her. Take away her pain. Save her eyesight."

Next afternoon, when he arrived at her room, Ron wasn't prepared for the commotion he encountered. Walking up to the door he was certain he heard clapping and singing, as if it were a jam session. Sure enough! When he walked into her room he was engulfed in praise music.

To God be the glory,
Great things he has done,
So loved he the world
That he gave us His son

Who yielded his life
An atonement for sin,
And opened the lifegate
That all may go in.

Praise the Lord, Praise the Lord,
Let the earth hear his voice!
Praise the Lord, Praise the Lord,
Let the people rejoice!

O come to the Father, through Jesus the Son,

And give Him the glory, great things he has done.

Ron misunderstood the attitude of praise.

He was instantly ecstatic.

Obviously, he thought, as evidenced by all the excitement, the doctor had changed his opinion. Ron pushed around the worshipers with the Hallelujahs on their lips and stepped to the edge of the bed.

His expression sagged. He was shocked. Instead of her big brown eyes looking up at him, huge gauze pads were taped over both sockets. She couldn't see a thing.

Audrey's roommate leaned over to speak into her ear to be heard above the praises, "Ron's here."

"Ron!" Audrey said adoringly as she lifted her right hand toward space to hopefully touch him.

He took her hand in his and crouched down low to speak; but as he did, the singing stopped and his first words were thunderous, "I don't understand . . .

"I don't understand," he repeated in normal voice. "When I heard all the praising I figured you must already be well, but . . ."

She squeezed his hand firmly, understanding his dilemma as a nonbeliever. "The doctor wasn't very hopeful when he came in early this morning. The swelling is just too severe for him to check my vision. So he put these bandages on both eyes to protect them from any possible further strain. He should have a clear prognosis by the end of the week."

She smiled in affirmation. "But I already know. I believe God will restore my vision."

"Amen! Amen! Praise the Lord!" Her room full of friends chorused variously.

Ron was speechless. He could not agree with such a radical, non-scientific view. Nor, at the same time, could he discredit or belittle their faith.

Day after day he made his pilgrimage to the infirmary and the scene never varied. Christian friends attended her constantly with singing and clapping and faith-building praise. The attitude of the believers, rather than diminishing, reached out in ever growing assurance that a miracle of healing already had taken place.

Such faith in visible action is contagious. It got to Ron. Walking back to his dormitory that second day his mind could not escape the contrast between the praises for God in Audrey's room and his own language habits. He made a decision. On the spot, he vowed, "No more profanity."

The next day he encountered two of his football buddies on the steps of the John Carter Brown Library. "Hey, how's Audrey doin'?" One asked him.

"Praise God, she's feeling better today," he declared.

The two looked at him suspiciously and responded, "Fine! Fine!" Then they beat a hurried retreat in the direction of the athletic field.

Ron walked slowly up the steps, glancing back over his shoulder at his friends, trying to figure out their weird reaction to him. Suddenly his face broke into a beaming, natural smile. He could hardly believe it himself. For the first time in his life he had publicly honored God.

Gradually God himself took a direct hand in discipling the young athlete. The changes weren't dramatic or earth shattering. No one else took much notice. But Ron knew he had turned a definite corner.

The doctor took the bandages off at the end of the week and made a complete examination. He was amazed. He then knew what several dozen Christians had known for days: there was no significant, permanent damage to her eyes. Her vision was 20/15. Two tiny scars were the only lasting evidence that anything traumatic had happened.

"They're sort'a like beauty marks," Ron assured her.

"Oh! I'm so thankful that they're there," Audrey said firmly. "I don't ever want to forget this lesson. I really believe God allowed this to happen in order to correct me. I was becoming too lax in my walk with Him. This has jarred me back to a determination never to fail Him again."

Her words, "in order to correct me", seared themselves

into Ron's spirit. As a nonbeliever, looking from the outside, he couldn't see any room in her for improvement.

But he could see plenty need of change in himself. If God had indeed corrected this precious young woman so sternly, what horror must be in store for a wretch like him.

Ron quit hanging out with the guys so much. In the midst of a party he would look around and realize that something vitally important to him was missing. "I wish Audrey were here," he would complain quietly to no one and chastise himself for choosing to be there rather than with her and the God squad.

Increasingly he was aware of the gentle tug of God on his life.

However, he did not know how to respond. Or even if he should. His thoughts were consumed with the prospects of the NFL draft. That was of greatest importance to him. God would just have to wait.

Chapter 9
FIRST THINGS
FIRST

● ●

Gaining even a reserve position with a professional football team is accomplished by only a few hopefuls. It's not quite as easy as applying for a job at a nearby Wendy's. It is likewise even tougher than seeking a hard to find residency position at a major hospital after completing a grueling program of medical studies. More precisely, the process is similar to what a grade "A" hog goes through in order to become breakfast sausage: it is highly sacrificial in nature. It's a hard-nosed business in which men in management smile at young athletes who anxiously await a chance to grab the brass ring—and do so quickly if it is offered. No personal consideration is allowed to interfere or get in the way. The human elements, based on emotions, are cast aside, and ignored. This is the real world. A twenty-two-year-old should be man enough to face up to a competitive and disgustingly impersonal bidding war as to his physical talents and the stamina of his character. He is tested, timed, and examined as a hunk of flesh. Then put on the auction block, much as if he were being judged for a Kentucky yearling sale.

From early in his junior season, for more than a year, Ron had been contacted by pro scouts from most of the 28 NFL teams. At times they sought his favor. In other instances they brushed past him to someone else as if he didn't even exist. The inconsistency of their attitude toward him kept him on edge—sometimes up, sometimes down. One particularly hopeful instance was right after the season finale against Columbia, his last game as a college athlete. A scout for Cincinnati said he would surely be drafted and that the Bengals were interested in him. It was the closest thing to an absolute offer he'd heard, though not an outright confirmation that he was pro material. There were other scouts who spoke in general terms about free agency.

With the end of the season, there was also an end to the almost steady, regular praise he had received from his coaches, the fans, and the press. All the glory quickly faded into a dim history. He was no longer a college athlete. That was over. A new phase of life was about to begin. The big question now—was he pro material or not?

Would any team want him? He hoped so. How he wished it! But because of the stress of the mind games the scouts played with him for months, he just didn't know.

Ron was so uncertain of what might come to pass that he intelligently kept one eye on graduate school. Come what may, he intended to pursue a masters degree in hospital administration. As a hedge against the future, in case he didn't make it as a pro, he applied to Columbia University.

Ron, always anxious to please, never wanting to offend, was a hapless target for a rare breed of opportunity seekers who year-in-and-year-out stalk the locker rooms of college campuses—professional agents. Like most other seniors eligible for the NFL draft that year, Ron very much wanted to make a team but was flush with a hundred questions as to how it happens. And just as surely as salmon go up river to spawn, every year would-be agents descend on college athletes to offer their services as a buffer between the athlete and the "big bad owners" of teams. Some are knowledgeable, honest, and sincere. Others, however, are pure and simple fortune hunters—seeking only to grab a quick buck and run.

Enter the agent.

"Hello, Ron, my name is Gus Dowling. I'd like to take you out to dinner tonight to talk about being your personal agent for your professional football career."

Gus was the first agent to approach him. And being interested in getting some answers to his many questions, Ron readily agreed. Dowling selected the finest of the many fine seafood restaurants in the city. During the meal Ron was impressed with the man's mild manner, it fit his own style nicely. He enjoyed the small talk as they got acquainted.

Then Dowling got down to business. "I've been watching your career closely for quite some time, Ron. Now that the draft is only a few months away I'd like to team up with you as your agent.

"I already represent a number of players on several different teams. So team owners and scouts recognize me as a tough negotiator."

Though he was talking about himself Dowling's words didn't sound like bragging. He was a man of the world. He spoke fast. Confident.

Ron was overwhelmed. He was also flattered that someone who was already in the big time, as an agent for NFL players, wanted to represent him as well. "I'm pleased that you want to represent me, Mr. Dowling..."

"Gus!" He interrupted with emphasis.

"All right, Gus," Ron continued agreeably. "But, tell me, what can you do for me as an agent that I can't do for myself?"

"That's a good, intelligent question," Gus replied. "It's not so much what I can do for you, but what more can we accomplish working together as a team—after all any final decision is always yours. My responsibility is to bargain in good faith on your behalf."

"Well, I certainly could use some help in knowing what to do," Ron admitted. "But," he continued awkwardly, not wanting to sound too mercenary, "how much is it going to cost to have you represent me? I know you guys don't work for free."

Gus laughed good naturedly. "You're right that I don't work for free. But my pay actually comes out of the owner's back pocket.

"You see," he continued in confidential tone, "since I've been through the procedure time and time again I know what to ask for and how to get it. I'll be able to get you a higher signing bonus and, through negotiations, a better first year salary.

"I may be able even to get you selected in a higher round.

"Now my fee is just three percent of whatever you get. That's why I say that since I can get you more, you actually don't pay me anything—it's almost like an added fringe benefit.

"And I'll get more of those for you, too!"

Ron studied carefully the contract Gus Dowling laid out on the table in front of him. It was spelled out clearly that if Gus failed to negotiate a satisfactory contract for him, he owed the man nothing. That provision, more than anything else, lured him into believing everything else the man had claimed about himself. Ron's palms sweated. He was ripe with excitement as he pondered what to do.

He signed.

After he returned to his room Ron read through the details of the contract again and again. At last it struck him clearly that it was for real. Finally! He knew he was on his way. From that point forward his confidence level jumped noticeably. He had nothing to fear. His agent, who should know better than anyone else, assured him, without qualification, that he would be drafted somewhere between the fourth and tenth rounds.

"In fact," Dowling had concluded, "I wouldn't be surprised if you went in the third."

For the moment Ron was elated. The fact of having a contract with an agent, however, left him with only momentary satisfaction. As the days of waiting for the draft turned into weeks he became more and more sullen.

"What've I gotten myself into?" He mused. "Yes! I have a valid contract with an agent—whom I've never heard of before.

"But a man doesn't play in the National Football League

for an agent! It takes a team contract!"

Would he rather have a team or an agent?

His emotions churned in turmoil throughout the long days leading up to the draft.

He prayed. But that was of no discernible help. He didn't believe in supernatural intervention anyway, although he was still bewildered by Audrey's "unexplainable" recovery. He was sinking in his spirit, tossed back and forth by every changing wave of the moment. He went to church twice. Yet he found no relief there. It was a profitless exercise. He heard nothing that was said or sung because he spent every minute recalling the names of every draftable player he could bring to mind.

Meticulously he matched each of those mighty men, one round after another, with various NFL teams. Then equally as methodically he redrafted everyone again. Over and over he continued the ridiculous numbers process endlessly.

As draft day approached, Ron had lots of well wishers, both by telephone and in person. But their words of encouragement were of only passing value, empty of substance. Daily, all they said disappeared from his mind as quickly as the sun hid from the earth. It was the long intervening hours that gave him the greatest stress. The intense internal insecurity, which he kept hidden from the view of others, haunted him throughout the night hours.

Audrey was his only anchor as he was tossed back and forth on the ebb and tide of his emotions. Her consistency of faith and cool demeanor helped him to hold somewhat steady. "Ron, I know how important being a pro football player is to you," she affirmed, as they arrived back at her dormitory after dinner one evening. "But, I also know something even more important! You must believe me that when the time for decision comes, God is going to be right there to help you.

"Listen to what it says here in Proverbs 3:5-6," she said as she reached for her ever present Bible.

Trust in the Lord with all your heart
and lean not on your own understanding;
in all your ways acknowledge him,
and he will direct your paths.

"That's the key, Ron, you have to trust in Jesus!"

He listened carefully to her words, but they seemed not to penetrate. Nothing brought relief. He wanted only to be wanted by some professional football team. He didn't care who—just so he was drafted.

It seemed to Ron that the momentous draft day would never come. Then when it did arrive he wanted to crawl deep under the covers and hide. Some college athletes, so sure of themselves and ready to celebrate, ganged up with others around America to listen to every detail of the draft broadcast. Not Ron Brown. He wanted to be alone.

As the drama of the draft unfolded there were no early surprises. As widely expected, Tom Cousineau, a linebacker from Ohio State, was taken number one by the Buffalo Bills. Then, on and on it went. Painfully slow. When the third round ended without the mention of his name and selections moved into the fourth round Ron began to pace the room. He hadn't listened to any of the introductory proceedings. Not expecting his name to come up in the early going, he had gone out to shoot baskets to ease the tension. Yet that brought no relief. He was nervous inside and out. With each succeeding opportunity he was baited with excitement to hear his name. But, alas, his name was ignored through the fourth round, the fifth, and the sixth as well.

The first day of the draft was over.

His stomach churned in anguish. He sat down to listen intently to the conclusion of the broadcast. But he couldn't relax. He stood.

Impossible, horrendous thoughts bombarded his brain. "What if I'm not drafted at all? What if nobody picks me?"

He paused and caught a glimpse of himself in the mirror. He turned, leaned heavily with his outstretched hands on the dresser top, and looked at himself blankly. Unappreciatively he considered the youthful face, topped with close cropped hair. He tried to look inside himself. He could see nothing. Nothing!

Ron slept poorly that night. His name had not been even hinted at. The final six rounds of the draft loomed ahead.

Next morning he lay in bed as long as he could to put off the day's proceedings. After a long shower he flipped on the radio for the start of the broadcast. In his ears the din of the draft dragged on—and on. Words seemed to mingle meaninglessly with others. Names of players he never heard of were coughed up from colleges he'd never heard of. It appeared to him that scouts must have gone all the way to Mars to find someone to be inserted into a draft slot which should have been his. He wanted to hear every name, yet he wanted to hear none of them. Most of all he wanted to hear his own name. When were they going to get around to Ron Brown of Brown?

Each selection created excitement. Everyone on radio was expressing congratulations to others. They were happy. But there had to be some mistake, Ron kept insisting to himself! Still, they had missed the All-Conference defensive back from Brown University.

Ron felt empty. Yet, at the same time, as his emotions churned he felt nauseous.

He laid down on his bed. He stared at the ceiling. He wanted to block out the draft from his mind. Yet he did instant replays in his mind. Surely he had missed something. He lay quietly for a long time.

"No! I haven't missed anything!" He whispered to himself. "I just won't be chosen!"

His spirit sagged with the thought of giving up his dream.

He wanted to cry, but was ashamed to do so even in private.

"What can I ever do?" he asked the ceiling. "All I have dreamed of and worked for these last five or six years has been to play pro football."

But the ceiling ignored him as surely as the draft was doing. It stared blankly back at him.

Far from his mind were any positives of life. He was totally oblivious to the fact that he had accomplished a quality education and that he would be graduating in a couple of weeks. Such thoughts were far from him.

He wanted only to belong to a professional football team. There was no one present to give any promise or answer to his inward yearning. He was struck by the overwhelming silence of the room. For that matter, the entire building, the university, the world seemed to be in a trance with him.

A sudden jarring ring of the telephone snapped him back to reality. His first thought was to ignore it. He wanted to speak to no one.

It rang again. "Maybe it's my worthless agent! Where was he when 28 teams spent two whole days selecting every athlete in the country—except me."

He let it ring.

Persistently the phone demanded an answer a third and fourth time. "Hey, maybe they're calling with my draft notice," he declared aloud as he swung his feet over the side of the bed and reached for the receiver.

Suddenly Ron thought he saw light at the end of the tunnel.

"Hello," he said hesitantly.

"Hello, Ron. This is Joe Roush of the Dallas Cowboys."

Ron's eyes lit up. Thankfully he hadn't been forgotten. He'd been drafted after all. "Hey, Mr. Roush, are you drafting me?" Ron asked bluntly, brightly.

"Well, Ron, as you know the draft is about over—and it doesn't seem like anyone is going to select you. But we'd like to sign you to a free agent contract."

The bottom fell out of Ron's life a second time. He was sorry that he had blurted out something so sophomorish and stupid over the telephone. He was thankful at least that no one could see him squirming like a worm within himself.

"Well, I don't know. To tell you the truth, I feel a bit down right now." Ron responded honestly.

"You wouldn't be human if you didn't feel low," Roush observed. "But come on down to my hotel and let's have lunch and talk it over."

Pride wanted to hide. Ego wanted to say no. But the desire to play pro football said, "I guess so. Where are you staying?"

"I'm at the Marriott. Tell you what. How about if I pick you up in front of your dorm in say an hour?"

"Sure. OK. I'll be ready," Ron agreed.

With that he flipped off the radio. He had no desire to hear the conclusion.

As he walked down the stairs and waited on the steps for the rendezvous Ron was glad the place was rather deserted. He didn't want to see anyone he knew. He didn't want to have to explain why he wasn't drafted. Nor did he fancy listening to someone fumble for words to try to console him.

"Being a free agent isn't so bad," Ron reasoned to himself. "I'll get a chance to go to the training camp and earn a spot on the team.

"Several free agents make it in the NFL every year.

"And the Cowboys are 'America's Team'. More free agents make their team than any other squad in the NFL."

Ron was feeling much better about the whole affair when Roush picked him up shortly before one o'clock.

The noon crowd at the Marriott restaurant had thinned out considerably when they arrived. Throughout the meal Roush talked glowingly about his view of free agency and what advantage the Cowboys had gained by their selections.

"Ron, we're going to be choosy. We'll only sign contracts with twenty-three free agents. From those—along with our twelve draft picks, last year's veterans, and the off season trades—will come next fall's squad.

"Ron, I realize how you and other athletes agonize through the drafting process—and not to be selected is tough. But, being a free agent is actually better than being a late round pick. This way you can select any team of your choice. Which gives you better negotiating power.

"And your chances of making the team aren't much diminished."

Ron gained a perspective on the draft proceedings from management's viewpoint that he hadn't considered before. He relaxed as they talked, and ate heartily to make up for the near fast he had endured during the draft.

As he enjoyed the last bit of dessert, Roush pushed the pie plate to the edge of the table and produced a contract. "Now it's time to get down to business, Ron. The Cowboys think you have talent and we'd like to give you a chance. This is our standard free agent agreement. We pay your expenses while in camp. If you earn a spot on the team we guarantee a three year contract with performance incentives and built in cost of living increases.

"All you have to do is sign here on page three."

"Well, I'd like a day or two to think about it—and talk it over with my agent."

"Ron, I doubt that you'll ever hear from that man again. There was nothing in your contract with him that gave you any guarantees. Right now, I imagine, he's out scraping the barrel, looking for someone who was drafted—and who needs an agent.

"Listen, I don't want to sound blunt; but there are a lot of good players around the country who weren't drafted. We can't afford to give you a lot of time to make up your mind while some competing team grabs up the others. So, here's the contract. Sign on the dotted line, or we'll go ahead and offer it to somebody else."

Roush might have disclaimed not wanting to sound blunt, but for sure, Ron knew how a bull feels in a slaughter house when struck between the eyes with the full force of a sledge hammer. He reeled inside from the emotion of the blow.

"Will you excuse me for a moment," Ron blurted out as he stood from the table. He was so disappointed he didn't know what to do. He left the man sitting there and pushed himself around tables and chairs and into the hall. "That's great!" he mumbled to himself. "Here I am! I've worked twenty-two years, all my life, to be the best athlete I could be. I wanted to be in a position where I could have a chance to maybe try professional sports. Now this guy, a total stranger no less, shoves a contract in front of my face and says sign on the dotted line—or else."

Once in the hallway Ron had no direction as to where to go. So he just stood there. The lunch hour was over. He had the corridor pretty much to himself.

He searched for an intelligent thread of thought to cling to. His mind was blank. He felt purposeless, adrift on an uncrossable sea. He stood in silence for several moments, his back against the wall.

Suddenly a name flashed in his mind. A name he hardly knew. A fresh name. He thought of Jesus Christ.

Like a gentle flow of spring water over thirsty ground that name brought refreshment to his troubled mind. Slowly he recalled from the preceding three years the bits and pieces of testimony he'd heard from a dozen different mouths. The words even of nameless God squaders melded into one intelligent message of love and hope and concern.

A relaxing smile creased his face as he thought again of Harry Walls and all that the man's life stood for. He wondered for a moment what Harry, always so positive in his outlook, would say at a time like this. Immediately a response filled his heart. He knew that the man would have words of praise and encouragement for him.

In the quietude of the hall his thoughts focused on Audrey's last words to him, "Ron, you have to trust Jesus." He began to realize that was an affirmation to the often asked questions, "Do you love the Lord? Are you willing to follow the Lord?"

He sensed with stunning appreciation that he was not alone in the hallway. He was comforted. He began to speak earnestly, inwardly, with but a slight movement of his lips, to an Unseen Presence.

"Lord, you know my outward appearance looks good to a

lot of people. I'm fooling a lot of folks. I'm fooling all the old people back home. They think I'm a fine upstanding young man. I'm fooling all my friends back home because even though they think I'm a coach's pet and a teacher's pet they have respect for me. I know that..."

Unconsciously tears welled up in his eyes.

"And I'm fooling all these people here in college. Yeah, I'm the class clown! And I look like I'm happy and having a good time. On the outside it looks like I'm doing well in school and sports! But on the inside my life is misery. It's a pressure cooker."

He gasped in anguish and wiped away a trickling tear.

"There are other people in the world who are going through a lot more hardship than Ron Brown is." He paused at the horror of the thought. "But at this moment, in this time, I feel worse than anybody in the world!

"I feel alone!

"Lord, I need you!"

At once, Ron knew that he had crossed a threshold. He entered into a sanctuary. That which he had rejected so forcefully for so long became his throbbing desire. With a seriousness of intent which he had never experienced before he asked Jesus Christ to come into his heart.

Not with a flow of poetic words, but with sincerity he declared, "Jesus, I've heard a lot about you, but I don't know exactly what I'm doing. Up to now I haven't paid close attention. I don't know a lot about you. But I do know I need you in my life. And I'm going to follow you whatever it takes—and wherever you take me!"

That was a complete reversal of field for the "I Can Kid", the one who had professed to have all the answers. All at once he knew that he didn't know anything. He had made a gigantic commitment. Not only had he climbed willingly into the wheelbarrow of the Master. He had done so as a blind man. He had no spiritual sight by which to judge.

All his life he had believed in God. He had known that God was out there somewhere, controlling things. He realized he had been protected at birth, and as a kid from spending life on the streets. He knew that it was God who had brought him to a good home, a disciplined home where he was fed and brought up well. God had given him a chance to go to college and play football, something he loved to do. God had given him a good life. He believed all that.

But when the great crunch of life came, intellectual assent of God's existence was not enough. He needed something more on which to bank his life. He made his first deposit in trust to God. He reached out in faith with a decision for a working relationship with the Almighty.

Committing his life to Jesus Christ in that hallway was an intimate, personal experience. The most satisfying moment of his life. Far greater than any sporting thrill. In the twinkling of an eye he stepped from darkness into light. And he knew it!

Having taken care of the most important matter of life, he was ready to go back and face Joe Roush and the matter of pro football.

As he returned to the restaurant he wondered if one of those miracles that Audrey and others talked about would now unfold for him. Those fifteen or twenty minutes of time had changed the whole direction of his life. In the meantime had God changed the mind of Roush and the Dallas Cowboys? Was an honest-to-goodness monied contract waiting for him?

He sat down across the table from the middle aged scout. He looked at the free agent contract. Nothing had changed.

"I think it would be wise for me to talk to my agent," Ron said with a new found confidence.

"Fine. I'll be glad to talk to him as well," the scout said. "Let's go up to my room to finalize this."

From there Ron called his agent to explain the offer.

"Let me handle this," Dowling advised.

Ron handed the receiver to the scout who was lounged in a chair. Amazed at the rancor between the scout and his agent, Ron listened to one end of the conversation. It quickly degenerated into a heated argument about dollars. The scout was insistent, "We can give Ron no guarantees! How long have you been in this business, Dowling? Don't you understand that there are no assurances attached to free agency. If he makes it—then we negotiate."

There was silence in the room as the agent responded. Harsh murmuring was all Ron could overhear from the receiver.

"Dowling!" Roush spoke evenly into the telephone, with emotion. "I've been with the Dallas organization for ten years. In that time I've seen your kind come and go. The dollar sign is all you think about. You make big boasts to impressionable kids. But you're not interested in the game or the players. I wish we were rid of the likes of you."

The two hung up in anger.

Understanding the uncertainty through which Ron was going, the scout called Dallas to explain the stalemate to his boss, John Wooten. Then he handed the telephone to Ron.

Wooten in turn repeated the previous ultimatum to Ron, "We have to have your decision now! If you don't sign we have to look elsewhere quick. I know this is not the easiest decision you'll ever make, but it's not the hardest either."

"Go ahead and sign the contract Roush has for you."

Ron stared at the papers in front of him for several minutes, trying to study them, but not really able to concentrate. To make matters worse the scout kept applying pressure.

"Listen, Ron," Roush finally declared. "We need to wrap this up. I'm going to call the home office again to see if they think I should hang on any longer."

Roush talked for a couple of minutes, explaining the situation. Then he held the receiver out to Ron, "Gil Brandt the General Manager of the Cowboys wants to talk with you."

Somewhat surprised by the opportunity to talk with the great Gil Brandt, Ron said, "Hello."

"Ron, this is Gil Brandt. I understand you have some

uncertainty about our free agency offer. Your agent called me after he talked to you. He's very upset. I told him, that at this point, the decision is up to you. I want you to know Ron that you were in our draft plans, but you were just down the list too far. But we have great confidence in your ability and would like to give you a chance to make the team.

"I hope you'll decide to give us a try. But take a few hours to think it over."

As he recradled the telephone Ron was relieved and impressed. The man understood!

Later that evening he signed.

He returned to the seclusion of his dormitory room to think through the day's events.

He'd just begun to relax when a scout for the New England Patriots called. "Ron," he said anxiously, "Where have you been? We've tried to reach you all afternoon."

"I just got back from signing a free agency contract with the Dallas Cowboys."

"That's too bad," the man admitted woefully. "You were in our plans as well. But the best of luck to you, Ron."

Ron learned shortly that negotiating in the National Football League is a hard fought business. Joe Roush had performed his task for the Dallas Cowboys in perfect style. Even before the draft was concluded he threw out his bait to his target; and then got him away from his own telephone in order to control the situation.

Not only had the Patriots tried, in vain to reach him, but other teams had sought him out as well.

Yet Ron had no regrets. He had a free agent contract in his pocket, primarily due to the gentle persuasion of the renowned Gil Brandt.

But! Far surpassing that, or any other prize, he had a new covenant with God in his heart. That was not due to any act of man. It was a result solely of the remarkable, gentle, persistent wooing of the Holy Spirit. That contract, inscribed in his heart, was not provisional. He did not have to prove himself. God and he were bound in an eternal plan. Heaven or hell was at stake. Ron Brown was heaven-bound.

Chapter 10
DREAMS ARE HARD TO COME BY

● ●

Just the privilege of finally signing a professional football contract, even as a free agent, proved to be a satisfying experience. As Ron laid in bed later that final night of the NFL draft he was so excited that sleep was beyond his grasp. It had been an unbelievable day. He had made two awesome, gigantic decisions in tandem with one another! As his mind flowed like the constant slapping of ocean waves it was impossible not to tie the two together. He speculated: had God planned a spectacular, successful professional career for him as a testimony to thousands?

Visions of bone crushing tackles and high leaping interceptions churned through his whole being in those early morning hours. This went on in spite of the fact that Audrey had cautioned otherwise. After signing the Dallas contract he had made a beeline for Audrey's dorm to tell her every detail about the proposal from the Cowboys. More importantly, sitting on the couch in the lobby, he shared the joy of his commitment to Jesus Christ.

As he repeated the words of his simple prayer, tears coursed down her cheeks. She put her arms around him in a gentle embrace. A long minute passed. No words were exchanged. The moment was so special neither of them wanted to intrude upon it.

At length, Audrey spoke softly, her chin tucked over his shoulder, "Ron, I have prayed for your salvation so specifically for so long. Now I find it hard to believe that it has finally happened. I am so very happy."

Taking her by the arms he pushed her back slightly to look directly into her eyes. "Audrey, I can never thank you enough for all your prayers and encouragement. I owe you a lot. I will never forget the thrill I had in the Marriott hallway when I realized that Jesus was real—just like you and others have been trying to tell me. But! Now I have experienced it for myself! Jesus Christ is truer than true. I've had hundreds of great highs in sports, but nothing can compare to that first moment of knowing him."

They eyed one another closely—communicating in spirit. Then Ron continued, "You know, then, signing that contract seemed just the right thing to do."

"I agree," Audrey affirmed. "I believe that's God's plan for you."

"Man!" Ron declared. "I feel just great. You know, this morning as the draft was coming to a close I felt lower than a worm under a rock. I felt that life was over. I just wanted to hide.

"When that scout called, I didn't even want to meet him. I felt even worse when he pressured me to sign that contract quick before he gave it to someone else. I was angry. I thought, 'Why has life fallen down on top of me?' I felt crushed. I just wanted to get out of there and avoid life.

"I only got as far as the hallway when I said to myself, 'OK, Brown! Where are you going to run to?'

"I was stumped. Cornered."

He paused in happy reflection.

"Then! There he was. Jesus Christ. As if he had been waiting in that hallway all eternity for Ron Brown to come to an end of himself! Jesus was there. And I knew it. And we made a deal. Praise God! We made a deal."

"I'm so happy for you," Audrey interjected. "But this is probably a good time to remind you of what the pastor said in church last Sunday."

"What was that?" Ron questioned.

"Remember, he said, 'Becoming a Christian is one of the easiest things in the world to do, but living the Christian life is one of the hardest things.' Ron," she continued, "it's not going to be easy for you in Dallas."

"Are you kiddin'?" He asked with a chuckle. "I know I have to keep making the right kind of choices, but it's so obvious that God is in this whole thing. Surely He's going to use my talent on the football field to bring honor to Himself."

The next week Ron was off to Dallas for the Cowboys' tryout camp. Much to his chagrin, as he got acquainted with others, he found out that he was surrounded by not just 22 other free agents as Joe Roush had promised. There were more than a hundred who had signed on the same dotted line. The Cowboy's obvious intention was to have a first look at them. Effectively, all that potential talent was safely tucked away from other teams.

Ron tried to act nonchalant. To take all the excitement in stride. But being in the same locker room with such stars as Tony Dorsett, Roger Staubach, Cliff Harris, and Charlie Waters was a heady experience. Here were men who had more than mere raw talent. Here were men who had achieved success in a grueling arena. Rather than being overwhelmed and intimidated by such giants of the game, however, Ron was determined to emulate them. He too would set high goals and attain them. He would look good, be a good player, and set a good image.

In the first days of training camp the workouts are not too strenuous since most players have taken time off and need to sharpen their skills. Emphasis instead is on technique and assignments.

After just a couple of days Coach Tom Landry sent word for Ron to meet him in his office. Ron was ecstatic. He knew he hadn't displayed anything special on the practice field yet, but evidently Landry had been looking over the scouting reports or had viewed highlights of some of his college games. "Oh, this is great!" He thought to himself as he headed to meet with the big man. "Landry wants me in his office. This can only mean that we are going to talk some serious contract negotiations."

He paused in his reveling to whisper a prayer, "Thank you, Lord, for giving me this opportunity."

Ron rolled into the office of the man who is a legend in his own time. Landry looked up from across his wide desk. His expression was calm as ever, giving no clue as to what was on his mind. But being a man of few words he came immediately to the point. "Ron, we're sending you home. I'm sorry to tell you that you flunked the physical."

The words hit him like a splash of cold water, quenching the fire of his spirit. Stunned, he asked, "Flunked the physical? How?"

"It's your right shoulder, Ron. It just doesn't stand up well under the stress tests," Landry advised matter-of-factly.

Determined to reverse a horrible decision, Ron responded, "Coach, I've never missed a game in all my life. Yeah, I hurt this shoulder a couple of years ago. I missed a couple of practices, but I never missed a game. You know, Coach, it just doesn't bother me that much."

Landry looked at him sympathetically. Being the bearer of bad news to athletes was one detail of his work that he detested. Nonetheless, it was part of the job. He said, "Ron, I appreciate that. But we have a policy that we just don't take guys we think are injured. We just can't afford to put you on injured reserve all season long—and pay you all season long for not playing all season long. So, we have to go ahead and cut you right now. That's just team policy."

So in a matter of hours Ron was "flying the friendly skies" back to Rhode Island.

Those were disquieting moments for the young athlete. His sports world, to which he had devoted himself so diligently, unsympathetically caved in upon him. For the second time in less than a month he had been rejected by the very thing that had given him meaning in life: first he had not been drafted, now even free agency abandoned him. Athletics had been his ticket to recognition, respect, and a college education. He had counted heavily on the prestige of at least six or seven years in the NFL.

"How can it be," he moaned to himself as he stared out the tiny window at the star studded sky, high above the clouds below, "that I flunked the physical? I've been in great shape all my life. I spent twenty-two years working out—to be at my best—and I go down there and fail a simple stress test."

He reasoned that he had given it his best shot. He was not at fault. But how could he explain this failure to his friends and family. Everyone had such high expectations for him. They had never seen him fail in anything he ever set out to do. Now he had to swallow hard, gulp down his pride, and face them.

"Why would God let this happen to me?" The newborn Christian asked himself in self pity. "What'll this look like to those who've heard about my commitment to Jesus?

"Lord," he cried softly through the gloom, "you know I only want to be a success to bring more glory to you."

No sooner were the words beyond his lips than he smiled to himself. He was new at the task of being a Christian, but he could almost hear God chuckling in response,"I have glory enough and enough to spare."

Because of the despair with which his trip began it was a long flight to Providence. But by the time the plane touched down God had spoken and given him a new definition of success. It was in stark contradiction to his former opinion of looking on the outside. "Son, what really counts with me is the inner man. I control the outer man. With or without an outstanding image on your part, I am in control. I have a different agenda than man. I'm more concerned with your inner being, your eternal soul. Let's work on shaping that up together!"

Though he was willing to learn from God, the first thing

Ron wanted to do, back in Providence, was to hide. It was far easier to face God whom he could not see than old friends he could see. He had begun to sort things out with God, but he was ill prepared to face friends—even Audrey.

But news travels fast. Bad news even faster.

The semester had not yet ended, and the Christians at Brown University were waiting for him. The distinguishing trait of true friends is their sensitivity when one is hurting. Ron's heart skipped a beat at his first sight of six of them waiting to greet him on the main campus green, with Audrey at the front of the pack. His mood shifted dramatically. He was instantly encouraged in spirit.

Audrey rushed forward to give him a kiss on the cheek, but Alfred Cummings squeezed in quickly between them and was the first to speak. "Hey, Ron, flunking a physical is nothing to be ashamed of.

"Look at me."

Everyone, even Ron, burst into laughter at the comparison—fat, blimpy Alfred and trim, muscular Ron.

The group joyfully pulled him to a quiet side of the grass and agreed together, "Let's pray about this right now. Ron, if God wants you to play football, or whatever he wants you to do in life, he'll heal you. He'll strengthen you. He will give you victory so you can do that."

Ron knew full well the type of victory they were talking about. The girl next to him, whom he loved, had miraculously recovered from her accident just six weeks earlier. He'd seen it with his own eyes. "That sounds good to me," he agreed. "That's the best news I've heard all week."

The answer to their praying was instantaneous. Ron knew God had healed him. Immediately he stopped doing special exercises for the shoulder and returned to a regular weight lifting routine as if he had a truly strong right shoulder.

The next week the semester ended. Audrey went home to New York City and Ron returned to the familiar surroundings of Martha's Vineyard.

In regard to old friends, his natural man wanted to hide

from them, to avoid the shame of having failed; but they seemed not to blame him.

Within a matter of days he began to relax from the strain he'd been under. Consistently he expressed his faith to the Lord that he was accepting God's healing touch. Amazingly, against all opinion of the Dallas doctor, his shoulder became steadily stronger.

A month later, in mid-June, he received a call from the New England Patriots. "Ron, we read the details about you being released from the Cowboys, but we would still like to take a look at you. As you know we tried to get you as a free agent on draft day.

"Why don't you come up and let our team doctor test you. If he gives you a clean bill of health we'd like to have you."

Ron packed his bags at once and headed for Foxboro.

At Schaefer Stadium, the Patriots' doctor put Ron through the exact same shoulder tests the Cowboys' physician had given him in Dallas. The man came out of the x-ray room shaking his head. "I don't know what the Cowboys' doctor saw," he declared. "but there's nothing wrong with your shoulder."

Ron signed a contract on the spot, in front of the Patriots' popular talent expert, Bucko Kilroy. Whatever the problem might have been it never bothered him again.

News of his second chance in the pros spread like wildfire across his island home. Once again he was a local hero—just like a light switch: then off, now on. Friends, even strangers, sought him out for an autograph—just in case he made it this time. One man, Kent Newsome, whom Ron knew slightly came to him with a special request. "Ron, I have a sixteen year old son who doesn't have any goals in life. Would you please take him out for a coke and just talk to him. He respects you and will listen to you."

Ron smiled sadly within himself, realizing the fickleness of sports fans. Just a few days earlier, before he had signed a new pro football contract, he hadn't been considered smart enough to tell anyone about the facts of life. Nevertheless, he gladly seized the opportunity and spent several hours talking with the kid.

Doubtlessly that encounter was good for the teenager, but it was equally important to the pro prospect. The counseling that afternoon set a life-changing pattern for Ron Brown. He loved the challenge of combining his Christian witness with athletics.

A few days later, as he drove to the Patriots' training camp, the miles melted away. He was full in spirit, "You know," he said to himself, "this Christian life is wonderful. When you first accept the Lord there is an instantaneous love relationship, a true love bond. You're really emotionally involved. It's marvelous.

"I know now what God is doing. He's been putting me through a little trial, but I'm going to make this team.

"Just like I've planned, I'm going to serve God while I play professional football."

He arrived at the Patriots' camp in great physical condition. He proceeded to work hard under the direction of the coaching staff.

Off the field, however, he was a different man. His roommate observed, "Man, all you ever do is read that Bible. Don't you think you ought'a be looking at the playbook some?"

But Ron found great comfort and security in God's Word. The playbook caused him nervousness and fear. He was no longer trying to put up a false front of self-confidence. He was beginning to face his own weaknesses.

He was studiously learning the Word of the Lord, on the one hand; but on the practice field he didn't know any of the Patriots' defensive strategies. He was out of balance.

Therefore, in spite of observing righteous practices, he fell into a devilish trap of being overly self-involved. On the playing field he was ill at ease, felt out of place and found it difficult to keep his attention on anything, God or football. Consequently, he began looking around at his competition in the Patriot backfield. Standout stars like Mike Haynes, Raymond Claiborne, Tim Fox, Ricky Sanford—all former number one draft picks—playing the same position as he. He began to worry, wondering how in the world he would make the team. His normal determination to succeed was swallowed by insecurity. His attitude to do well suffered and sank.

Naturally, his performance dipped markedly. Instead of concentrating on what God could do with his life and talents, he thought continually about the obvious ability of others. Comparing himself to them, he began to fail miserably.

Others noticed as well. The defensive backfield coach was constantly on his case. In desperation one day he screamed out, "Ron, you frustrate me! Here I am a Christian man and you're making me swear at you! You're just not concentrating and applying your talents!"

For the first time in his life he looked for an easy way out. "I can't handle this anymore," he confessed to himself. "Football's a crazy sport anyway. I was accepted at Columbia. I might as well go on, quit wasting my time, and become a hospital administrator."

After harboring that thought for several days Ron decided to test the waters. He would offer to pack it in. He was unsure of himself. Even so there was a hope within him that the coach would beg him to stay. Maybe coach would say, "Ron, you know, you're a pretty good player. I think you ought'a stick with it. You have great potential. Don't worry yet; it's still early."

Fresh from the showers that afternoon, Ron went up to the Patriots' head coach, Ron Earhardt and said, "Coach, I'm done. I'd like for you to put me on waivers and let me go."

Without a hint of remorse, Earhart responded, "Fine. Go."

So he quit that Friday afternoon.

The next morning, as he was packing his bags, the scout who had signed him walked by wordlessly.

A few minutes later, however, Raymond Berry, one of the Patriots assistants who had coached Ron on punt returns, came and sat down on the office couch next to Ron. Berry, in his playing career, had distinguished himself in the NFL as a Hall of Fame wide receiver; and also projected a solid Christian image.

"You're from Martha's Vineyard, aren't you?" The coach asked casually.

"Yeah," Ron answered singularly.

"I hear the fishin' down there is pretty good."

"Yeah," Ron agreed, "though I'm not much of a fisherman."

"Well, I'm sure its a great place to live," Berry affirmed understandingly. "I wish you the best. Take care of yourself."

"Thanks."

Ron sighed deeply as he watched Berry walk away. The man had gone out of his way to uplift the fallen. And he had left behind a real Christian witness without having used any religious words.

Ron called his folks to explain what he was doing; and headed for New York City, graduate school, and Audrey. She of course was returning to Brown University, but they had several days to talk and pray together before the start of the fall semester.

"I've got a new life now," Ron explained to her. "No more wastin' time on a football dream. I'm going to serve the Lord as a hospital administrator."

Audrey was disquieted in spirit, but expressed only mild reservations. She remembered so clearly the prayers of May, asking God to mend Ron's shoulder. Then the subsequent healing. She remembered his craving to be a pro football player. Then his elation at being invited to join the Patriots, his homestate team. But she wisely listened, giving no advice.

Ron also was ready for a commitment to the young woman. She, however, was not totally sure about that. She wanted to wait on God's definite guidance.

As Audrey left for Providence, Ron turned his attention to the demands of graduate studies. At the same time he became involved in working with young, underprivileged kids. One of the kids, a four year old named Nathan, became like a little brother to him. Nathan lived with his grandmother in a troubled section of Queens. His mom was in prison. His dad was on tough times. He was growing up like a wild weed between the cracks in the sidewalk. He often spent time in a dingy park across the street from his building, just walking around. He was emotionally disturbed and getting to the point, even at his tender age, where he'd be beyond help.

Ron spent a lot of his spare moments with the little boy with the big brown eyes. "Now, don't you let life get you down," Ron encouraged him as they sat on the curb one afternoon. "Remember, God is a big God and he can take you to great places. I know He can! Now, don't you ever give up on life."

Nathan looked up at the man who was the nearest thing to a father he'd known. His hero. Adoringly he said, "Someday I want to see you play football."

The words, though loving and well intentioned, shattered the man. Ron made no response. He reached out his big hand and tossled the boy's hair and laughed awkwardly. But he could not so easily brush away that simple sentence.

To himself he yelled out a challenge. "Brown, you ought to be ashamed of yourself. Does it take a four-year-old to jar you into looking at the facts? You're a coward! You gave up on football on your own. Not because the Lord told you to. You gave up football because you doubted yourself.

"Now, how do you have the gall to tell this kid to never give up? You quit football because you were constantly comparing yourself to others and didn't like what you saw.

"You've been rationalizing around life. You've been hiding. You've been trying so hard to fool people again. You're just pretending to be happy with the idea of being a hospital administrator.

"You know that's a lie. Every time it comes to mind you turn it off because you can't stand the thought. Hey! Man! When're you going to face the truth?"

After that flash of thoughts, Ron stood to his feet and said, "Good night, Nathan, I'll see you tomorrow."

As he rode the E Train from Queens to Lower Manhattan and then a local subway uptown to the Medical Center campus Ron became increasingly convinced that God had a message for him in the simple wish of the child. "I've been telling this kid that with God you continue, no matter what. You just don't give up on things. You have to keep on pushing. When the Lord tells you it's time to go somewhere else he'll make a way. But right now, on my own accord, I've gone out on my own and strayed from God's best plan.

"No more! I'm getting back on track!"

And he did! Almost like Rocky Balboa in the movies: up at five o'clock in the morning, drink a dozen raw eggs, play inspirational music and run, run, run. Ron started a daily pounding of the streets of New York City. He began a steady program of weight lifting, joined the track club, doing everything to get back in shape; while taking seven classes in graduate school. He signed on with the New Jersey Rams, a semi-pro team, to play in their regional games. It was a crazy schedule. Sometimes he thought he was out of his mind. Yet he knew he was doing it for the Lord. And at the same time he was growing in his faith with God and in relationship with others. He studied the Bible faithfully, claiming along the way the promise of Jesus in Mark 10:27:

"All things are possible with God."

He was strengthened in both body and spirit as that new attitude took hold and developed. He was doing it all. Rather, he was learning that God and he were accomplishing something special together.

Next on God's agenda for the former Brown University star athlete was a humility lesson. He started writing to NFL teams "asking" for a chance to prove himself. Rejection letters piled on top of one another. The standard response was thanks, but no thanks. Often not even a whole paragraph.

But Ron was persistent, pushing past his previous problem of pride, he would post yet another proposal.

The odds against a positive reply, of course, were astronomical. With colleges and universities grinding out a fresh batch of potential candidates each and every year, the pro teams could be selective.

Then in March, ahead of the drafting frenzy, a letter arrived from the New York Jets. Ron walked slowly up the steps to his dormitory room, reading and re-reading the return address. His adrenaline was pumping as he sat down on the couch and tore open the envelope. The message was plain and simple, "Ron, we remember you as a player back at Brown University and we would like to sign you to a contract. Please give us a call as soon as possible."

Instinctively Ron's lips uttered, "Praise the Lord! It's true, 'with God all things are possible'."

He realized that such an opportunity just doesn't happen. It was a blessing from God and he intended to make the most of it. He worked harder on his conditioning and got in perfect shape.

Again, his parents and friends back home, Audrey and the believers at Brown, and his newly acquired Christian friends in New York were enthused about his third chance in professional football. As he prayed about it he was certain that God had prepared a way for him to be a success at last.

When he arrived at the Jets' training camp he was lean and hungry and ready to go. He knew he had an excellent shot at making the team. His position was wide open. The Jets had just traded their starting free safety, Burgess Owens, to the Oakland Raiders.

Gone were his inhibitions. He was not comparing or contrasting himself with anyone. He was determined that he could beat out anyone for a position. Correspondingly, the practices went perfectly for him.

Right at the close of the third day, however, he heard something pop. He grabbed his right thigh as if such a quick reflex could revert the blowout of his quad muscle. But, to no avail. He winced in pain and started hobbling around. He tried to do some extra running, but the defensive backfield coach came over to him and advised, "Ron, you'd better stay off that for the rest of the day."

His thigh swelled considerably. For four days he was not able to practice and had to content himself with riding the stationary bicycle. It can be quite embarrassing, when you are a free agent rookie in pro camp, to spend four days not practicing. Other players, coaches, trainers look at you strangely.

He refused to let the injury get him down. He was going to make a success of pro football. He did a lot of praying too. Miraculously the leg healed itself. Four days later he was back into the practice rhythm and playing well.

Everything was on track for his first season in the NFL. Or so it seemed.

At six o'clock in the morning, the day before the first preseason game against the Giants, there was a knock at Ron's door. "Come on in," he moaned sleepily.

"Ron, Coach Michaels wants to see you in his office—and bring your playbook." The messenger declared.

Ron thought it was a little early to be going over plays, so asked, "Can I eat breakfast first?"

"Yeah," was the soulful reply as the young man ducked his head back out the door.

As he walked into the coach's office, Ron, now wide awake, was instantly reminded of the Tom Landry scene just fourteen months earlier. An anxious gnawing bit into the pit of his stomach. His brain did a quick re-interpretation of the words, "bring your playbook". That really meant "pack your bags".

Just as Landry had, Michaels remained seated for his unsavory task. Unlike Landry, though, his eyes were down, maybe to avoid the pain of seeing disappointment in the face of the likable young athlete. He said clearly, "Ron, we're sending you home."

"Coach," Ron asked with an unmistakable plea in his voice, "why're you cutting me a day before the first game."

"Ron," he said, still without looking up, "we just don't

think you're going to make the team. We'll put you on waivers. Maybe someone else will pick you up."

As he packed Ron realized that the early morning call was a bit of a nicety—a guy could get all his gear out of the way before others arrived and wouldn't have to go through the humiliation of facing the successful ones.

Shame was the only word Ron had to describe it as he headed home for Martha's Vineyard. Actually he would have preferred to have gone the other way—like to California. He was so down emotionally he wanted to roll way out of town, where nobody he knew would ever see him again.

That though was not possible. He was a man and had to face life. Not only that, but he was also maturing as a Christian and was certain that God had a plan. True, he was faced with a dark cloud of doubt, almost burdensomely. But he was at the same time sure that God wanted him to hold his head high as he walked patiently through to the answer on the otherside, somewhere.

God was dealing with Ron Brown's inner man, fashioning a victor to his pattern. The outer man, unfortunately, was still cluttered with visions of success, fame, and glory.

To Ron the trip home seemed endless. Once he was on his way he just wanted to get there. He sighed heavily for the security he had always known in his parents' home.

However, he was not prepared for his mother's reception when he walked in the door. Ever since his telephone call, Pearl Brown had worried about how torn up he must feel on the inside from being cast off by a third team after having worked so hard. She took one look at her dear son and could not control herself. She wrapped her arms around him and cried. Ron bit his lip, to restrain himself from joining in her tears. He patted her consolingly, "That's all right, Mom. I'm fine. Everything's going to be OK."

Ron was puzzled. What was he supposed to do with his life now? He certainly needed more time at Columbia to finish his master's degree. But more than that he wanted to be a pro football player.

He turned to the One who had become his primary resource. "God!" He prayed. "What do you want me to do? Still inside I have a desire to play football. Is that crazy? Most people think I'm nuts. I've had three chances at making it big—and nobody gets a fourth chance.

"What am I to do? Please give me a sign."

The next day Ron went out for a walk. He was conscious of being peered at by strangers. Word had spread fast across the tiny town. Every sports page in America prints a daily list of those who are cut from pro football teams. On that day, that little blurb in the morning paper was Ron Brown's only claim to national fame. The last time he'd walked down that street he was a success in everyone's eyes. He had just signed another pro contract. He was somebody to know. Somebody to take pride in. Everyone had wanted to talk to him. Now no one stopped to speak.

At last, though, from down the street Ron was relieved to see a familiar face. Kent Newsome, who had asked him to talk to his son, was headed his way. The man looked up when he was about twenty feet away. Ron started to wave.

Newsome looked at him, turned his head, and walked across the street. The man, who a short time before had valued him as one to inspire his son, now viewed him as too much of a failure to even speak.

In the first rush of the rebuff Ron was tempted to pity himself, but instead grabbed hold of another invaluable bit of instruction. "Father," he prayed within himself, "thank you for this lesson not to rely on the praise of men, but rather on your presence."

A few days later another incident sealed the lesson in place. Ron was eating in a restaurant with a workout partner. An intoxicated man he didn't even know came up to his table and said, "You're Ron Brown, aren't you?"

"Yes, I am," Ron responded.

"You stink!" The man declared as he staggered away.

Ron was glad for the end of summer and its woeful disappointments. He returned to the discipline of his studies in New York and the pleasures of rich fellowship within the Christian group at Columbia Medical Center. He also had one full day with Audrey before she left for Brown.

Football still was not a thing of the past for Ron. In spite of the repetitious failures, he was holding on to hope to make a success of it in professional football. He was down but not out. There could yet be a miracle come his way. He joined the Rams for a second season, in 1980, anything to keep close to the real thing. He had an outstanding year, played well, was selected for All Conference honorable mention, and started a Bible study among the Rams.

Ron's best game of the season was at Bridgeport, Connecticut. He'd been struggling with a heel injury, but could still run. He decided to dedicate the game personally to Jesus Christ, to play for his glory. It was the first time he'd done such a thing. The only goal being to conform closer to Christ's image. To play the game the way Jesus would play. He forgot all about the painful heel, his prior "failures", his loneliness. It went well. He had two interceptions and ten tackles.

In May of '81 Ron was contacted by yet another agent, from Buffalo, wanting to represent him. Why not, he thought. The agent arranged for Ron and several others to go to a Kansas City Chiefs' tryout camp near Philadelphia at Cherry Hill, New Jersey.

On the way the car broke down. There was Ron and the other athletes packing along Interstate 95 to get to a telephone. Naturally they arrived late. To boot, it was a rainy day. He had little time to prepare for the first test in the tryout, running the forty. He wasn't loose. Instead of his normal speed of 4.5 or 4.6, he ran a 4.8. Way too slow for the pros. He lost his chance.

After he returned to New York he lost his new agent as well. The man screamed through the telephone, "You didn't follow through. You just jerked it off." And that was it.

Bob Engle, the offensive coordinator for the Rams, however, was far more interested in seeing Ron make the grade. Engle, who in real life was the cover editor for Newsweek, was a closet football enthusiast. He had a genuine enjoyment in seeing others make it to the top. In mid-May he arranged another tryout for Ron with the Patriots.

It was a humbling experience for Ron to return to Schaefer Stadium where a year before he had walked away from a free agency contract. This time, however, he had a renewed confidence and determination. Six hundred athletes showed up, nearly a hundred of them were defensive backs, vying for the two defensive back positions the Patriots needed to fill.

The first elimination step was the forty yard dash. Ron was pleased to see that the timer was Raymond Berry, the Patriot's coach who had spoken to him with such understanding the day he'd been cut. Ron ran the 40 in 4.65. He went on to the bench press and passed. In the standing broad jump he covered thirty feet in three leaps. That's good. He was excellent in coverage of receivers: not one of his men caught a ball. He wound up as one of six final competitors, but was not one of the two signed.

Back in New York, on the surface, Ron had a lot for which to be thankful: exposure to a high grade of football, a wealth of excellent Christian friends, a satisfying ministry with needy kids, and a graduate degree almost in his pocket.

Underneath, however, he had two bothersome concerns: athletics and Audrey. She was constantly on his mind. Though he dated around, no one could match up to her, to their freedom of communication. He missed her. Unfortunately though, he knew she didn't miss him nearly as much.

But equally burdensome to him, were the recurring doubts he had about his true motive for desiring to make it big in pro football.

In his third year with the Rams their schedule became national rather than merely regional. It proved to be his best. He was chosen as captain, had four interceptions in one game and a total of seven by mid-season. Then, in a game at Newark he suffered a cartilage tear in his right knee. The doctor declared he'd never play again. However, Bob Engle got him in to see the New York Giants' team doctor, Kim Sloan. After orthoscopic surgery by Sloan, Ron was back playing in three weeks. He went on to be named to the Semi-pro All American team.

Meanwhile, he was finishing up his master's degree. A short time before graduation Ron decided to take a one day retreat—just he and God alone for a time of reflection and meditation. He knew a spot high above the Harlem River. There, on a rock overlooking the valley below he read his Bible and searched his heart.

He reasoned, "What's it going to take for me to admit defeat? I've failed three times in trying to make a pro football team. But does that make me a failure? What does the Lord really want from my life? Why am I in this world?"

He prayed, "God, I've searched the Scriptures and my own heart for purpose. I need to know what your definition of success is. I seem to be missing it. I have this yearning to play professional football. But can that be from you? I've been so close three times, and each time I thought you would bless me in it. Surely such an opportunity won't come around again.

"But, Lord, I have such a yearning to make it!"

He opened his Bible and read. He studied through the account of Abraham and his faith that God would bless him with a son—even when the wait seemed humanly impossible and endless.

As he continued in his private study, the message of Isaiah 26:3 seemed to come alive:

> You will keep in perfect peace
> him whose mind is steadfast,
> because he trusts in you.

"Lord, you know I trust you," he concluded. "So I will continue this course you have set for me."

He graduated shortly afterward, in May of 1982, with his masters degree from Columbia. The day was made special by the attendance of Irene Chase, then in her eighties. The woman who had worked so diligently in arranging his adoption twenty-four years earlier had watched his progress across the years with admiration. She took pride in his accomplishments in high school, at Brown University, and finally at Columbia: pleased to have lived to see yet another step in the life she had helped to save.

Unfortunately, Audrey was not there. She was struggling with her own career plans and simultaneously grappling with some difficult relationships. This had triggered a lot of unresolved conflicts from her childhood. She had finished at Brown and was home in New York City, awaiting her entrance into graduate school. But to Ron's telephone call she insisted, "I don't want you to come by."

He tried to get a valid reason from her, but the best she could offer was, "Ron, it's not you, it's me. I just have a lot of things to sort through."

From that point on they were no longer "buddies." The one whom God had used greatly to bring him to Christ began to move away from Ron emotionally. For Ron it was a rejection which stung more than the three pro football cuts put together. It could never again be quite the same.

Ron, however, didn't have time to go into a tailspin. A few days after graduation he received a telephone call from Chicago that stirred the slumbering chords of his athletic soul. Miraculously the Bears invited him to come to their mini-camp for a tryout, "We need a defensive back," they explained. "We have a prepaid plane ticket waiting for you at LaGuardia. A cab is on its way to pick you up. You have just an hour to make the flight."

A tear trickled down the cheek of the macho athlete as he recradled the telephone. "How can this be? I know I just talked to the man and this is no joke. What a great opportunity. God is blessing me beyond reason. Now! This must be the time for the success I've been seeking—God has been testing and teaching me through these other trials."

This was a case of Bob Engle's influence once again. He

had contacted the Bears when he heard they were looking for a man with Ron's particular talents.

"Can he run 4.6 and is he physical?" Were the only two questions they asked.

Engle assured them of Ron's abilities and sent them a game film to prove it. The film he selected was of the 1980 Bridgeport game, which Ron had dedicated to Jesus Christ. The Bears' coaching staff viewed the film and agreed that Ron was capable of playing their type of physical game.

He arrived at the Bears' camp with high expectations. The unsolicited invitation to even be there was interesting in itself. No! More than that it was unbelievable. Such a call just does not go out to a man who's been out of college for three years and who's not played a minute in a pro game.

On the first day of practice Ron was pleased with himself. They were doing some defensive back drills and he was in top form. But after practice he didn't know what to think when he saw the coach, Mike Ditka, headed his way. Three previous personal encounters with head coaches had been disastrous—and this time it was only day one of the camp.

Ditka, who was in his first year as coach of the Bears, came up to Ron and put his arm around his shoulder. "Ron," he said, "you don't look like a rookie. You look like a pretty good player. We watched some film on you before. You've got a chance. You've really got a chance."

"Thanks, Coach," he responded as Ditka walked away. Ron was flabbergasted. Such a compliment is almost never heard by a free agent. But of course, in a sense, he wasn't a rookie anymore. He'd been to lots of camps and had gotten better.

He was on top of the world.

On the second day of practice they were running more defensive drills. The kind Ron had been through a thousand times before. Expertly he went up to grab a pass in mid-air. But he came down with a crunch. His right knee blew out. He lay on the ground writhing in misery, looking up to a gathering circle of concerned individuals. Ditka, Buddy Ryan, and a crowd of Bears looked down at him. Their faces told a singular story, "Too bad, but that's it for him."

Ron looked beyond them to the blue sky above and asked, "Lord, why're you dangling the carrot stick? Why? Why're you doing this to me? You know I've been seeking you and I've been praying and I've been working awfully hard at it. I have a good attitude and I've turned my life around in your name. Why're you doing this? Why do you keep giving me a desire to keep on? Why don't you just give me a desire for something else?"

As they laid him on the stretcher and wheeled him off the field a heavy grey cloud drifted across the sky.

Chapter 11
GOD'S BEST
• •

Once again, Ron dreaded going back to his family and friends. A failure. A loser. He could imagine varied whispered conversations behind his back:

"Why's he continuing with this?"

"He's a nut!"

"Why doesn't he go on, be a hospital administrator? At least that would be steady. He should make some money, and get on with his life."

"Why does he insist on pursuing these childish games?"

"He'll never be a success!"

Though he received consistent support and understanding from his parents, Ron knew there was no way he could follow through with achieving his dream on the island. There were too many prying minds in the tiny community. He decided to return to the safety of anonymity in New York City.

Yet he didn't have to go alone. Inside his soul he felt that still small voice of the Lord saying, "Stay with it. Stay with it. There's a plan for you."

Ron secured a fund raising position at Columbia to help pay expenses while he concentrated on rehabilitating his knee: the Bears had promised to bring him back if his knee was restored fully. Or perhaps a fifth chance from elsewhere would come his way. If it did he wanted to be ready.

A professional spot in football was his primary purpose.

But he also blossomed in the task at hand, becoming a top fund raiser. He was promoted to assistant director of the office with responsibility for training and overseeing new employees. In terms of career, those under him were like Ron in many ways: aspiring actors, actresses, musicians, writers, and dancers—all waiting for their "big break". Without his realizing it at the time that became his first coaching opportunity. God's plan was at work.

In addition, the Columbia School of Public Health helped open another door. He was hired by Blue Cross-Blue Shield as a corporate fitness consultant. In front of their offices at 34th and Park Avenue in Downtown Manhattan, he gave noon hour seminars right out on the street with a microphone. While jumping rope he talked about fitness, diets, shoewear, and heart rate. The company promotion heralded him as a defensive back with the Chicago Bears. Blue Cross was excited with the response and intended to use him again the following summer. But when the time came, since they could no longer tout him as a pro footballer the company reneged on the promise.

Meanwhile he was in no condition to play the 1982 fall season with the New Jersey Rams. Instead they asked him to be defensive coordinator and defensive backfield coach. He had no desire to be on the sidelines. He wanted to play. Nonetheless, in order to stay involved he accepted the challenge. It also kept him in touch with the Rams Bible study which he'd helped get started back in 1980.

He gained respect at both work and play. But only in his relationship with God did Ron feel true satisfaction with life. That along with the bonding and support from the other believers kept him from sinking into despair. True, he was maturing as a Christian. God mattered most to him. But in what was next in order of importance to him he was a failure. He doubted that he would ever succeed in athletics. Yet, he could not turn his back on the dream of his youth. In spite of setbacks, football was still real to him.

Ron continued to work hard on bringing strength back to

his knee. As part of his training program for another try at
pro football he began running with an AAU track team in
Harlem called the Pioneers. It was an active and aggressive
program, highly competitive. It had to be. In New York City
there are lots of fast guys, on the outside looking in, wanting
a chance. So, in order to encourage as many kids as possible
to get off the streets and into action, membership in the AAU
was not required to be able to compete in meets.

Because of his fascination with speed, Ron took keen
interest in the hundred meter dash at one particular meet
held on Randalls Island. Four guys lined up for the race. Two
had paid their registration fee and belonged to the Pioneers.
The other two were cold, right off the street.

The four took the mark. The team members looked sharp
in their uniforms and regulation shoes. They totally
outclassed the other two in swimming trunks, running in
ragged tennis shoes. The gun sounded. Like a shot the two
ragamuffins were off. The team members saw only the
backsides of the street kids who finished first and second. The
two Pioneers clocked in third and fourth.

Ron was scanning the sports section of the newspaper the
next morning for the meet results. To his amazement, the
guys who finished third and fourth were listed as finishing
first and second. The other two runners weren't even
mentioned. At lunch he saw one of the other Pioneers and
asked, "How did the results of yesterday's 100 meter dash get
misprinted in the paper? I saw what happened and those two
street kids beat our boys by a full second."

"Well," his friend explained, "you see we let anyone run
in the races who wants to, but it only counts if they're on the
team."

That afternoon, on his way to the Rams' Bible study, Ron
thought through that contrast and the importance of being on
God's team. As he did so the Lord, brought a clear
understanding into his heart as to how it applied to him.
"You see, son," that now familiar inner voice explained,
"there are a lot of people in life who are running good races,

fast races. There are a lot of people in life who look like they're winning. Their business is an outstanding achievement. They are renowned world success stories. They have a nice home in the suburbs, wonderful kids, a beautiful wife or handsome husband, a great job, and they make a lot of money. They seem to be rolling along just fine in life.

"They may play in the NFL or NBA, or sing and dance on the stage or TV or movies.

"But, son, I have something better for you than that. I want you to get beyond that idea of success.

"More than being successful, I want you to be faithful!"

For the first time in his life Ron truly understood the difference. His heart had been searching for God's plan for two years, but his mind had been stuck in a worldly frame of what it means to be a successful person.

At the Bible study he recounted to the Rams what he had learned from the experience. "You see," he explained, "God has his own newspaper sports page. It's called the Book of Life. If you have not joined his team, then your race doesn't count. It's just like Jesus says in Matthew 7:21-23:

> Not everyone who says to me, "Lord, Lord," will enter the kingdom of heaven, but only he who does the will of my Father who is in heaven. Many will say to me on that day, "Lord, Lord, did we not prophesy in your name, and in your name drive out demons and perform many miracles:" Then I will tell them plainly, "I never knew you. Away from me, you evildoers!

"If we haven't made Jesus Christ our Lord and Savior, then we're not on the team. We could be running apparently faster than anyone else, doing things better than everybody else, but in the end it won't count. Our names won't show up in God's publication of the Book of Life. That means eternity in hell."

In his earnestness Ron had spoken just as significantly to himself as he had to the others. The analogy opened up a new freedom of choice for him in his own life. The pressure from the driving desire to succeed in the eyes of the world began at last to ease.

In another area of importance, Ron also settled into a trust with God concerning the woman for his life. The right lady would come along at the right time. He dated freely. Audrey faded from the picture. He thought of her often because she had made an invaluable contribution to his life, but the passion was gone.

Memories rushed to the forefront momentarily, however, when she called in early January, 1983. The sound of her voice was familiar, yet there was a faraway tone in her greeting.

"Audrey, it's great to hear from you," he responded. "How're you doin'?"

"Ronny, I'm OK except for one problem—and I called because I need your advice." Her speech was strained.

"Sure!" He pledged. "What is it?"

"Well, there's this guy I've been dating—his name is Ralph. We get along great most of the time. However, I just don't know what to do. He's not interested in spiritual matters at all."

Ron listened patiently through her problem. It was evident to him that she needed to forget Ralph and move on with her life. "Listen, Audrey, I think you need to take time out from whatever you're doin' to get back your focus on the Lord. You need to get your priorities in order. Then what you do with Ralph or grad school or anything else will fit in its proper place."

She thanked him politely, but he could tell she was disappointed that he'd not given the advice she wanted to hear. She had wanted license to do as she pleased; not to change direction.

He was sorry she was going through such a struggle, yet as he cradled the phone back on its holder a wave of peace washed his heart. He had faithfully repaid the debt to the one God had used so specifically in his life. He was set free from that tie.

Ron continued to train to get himself physically fit. As he did so he also strained to find a fifth opportunity in pro football. But he struck out on both counts. The knee never came around and consequently the search was in vain. No football team is looking for a hobbled defensive back.

The door was shut.

At least the door he wanted was barred. The door he had pounded on so relentlessly would not budge. It was locked.

Ron was confused and felt unsure of his purpose. Most of all though he had no desire to make a career step outside of football. However, because so many things were up in the air, he searched anxiously for different career options.

But without his designing it, another door into the fabulous football world opened.

Wondering as to where his future was going, Ron talked to Andy Talley who formerly was running back coach at Brown and then head coach at Villanova. Talley suggested that Ron give coaching serious consideration. "Ron, you would be good at it. Listen, I know that John Anderson is looking for someone at Brown. You ought to give him a call."

Ron followed the advice. The coach wasn't in when Ron called, so he left a message. Shortly the call was returned.

"Ron, this is John Anderson," the man on the telephone identified himself. "I'm glad you called. I'd like you to interview for a position on our staff here at Brown. I heard about your dilemma and wondered if you were interested in staying in football via coaching? I need a freshman coach. However, we need to talk about it and see how the interview goes first. You see, I have over 400 applications for the position from experienced college coaches out of work and former pro athletes wanting to get into coaching.

"Could you come up next week so we can discuss it?"

Ron was shocked by the suddenness of the invitation and responded with some hesitation. "Well, as you know, this call is unexpected. And I don't know what I want to do.

"But," he affirmed with a quick decision, "I'll be glad to meet with you to talk about it."

The intervening week was hectic. With all his other responsibilities Ron had little chance to think through the prospect of being a full-time coach. From his earliest days as an athlete he'd had no such desire. He wanted to be a player. That's where the glory is.

The evening before he was to meet with Coach Anderson he was studying the basketball scores on the sports page when a short article at the side caught his attention. It was set off in a bold bordered box and entitled with a question:

IS FLEETING FAME TOO HIGH A PRICE?

In America today macho image is one of the most compelling forces of our society. And of all such image makers none is greater than that of men who make up the National Football League. These stalwart figures of weekend glory in the gridiron battles are held in highest esteem, not only by the youth, but by a broad section of the adult population as well. They are honored in their communities, sought after by the mighty and the lowly, and hounded by the press for morsels of comment to foment ever more suspense for impending games.

From August, through a seemingly endless season, and on through a sometimes tiring series of championships, professional football players hold status against rumors of wars, a rising or falling economy, crime in the streets, and fights in the family.

America has a love affair with its football players and pay a handsome price to watch their mastery of talent. But what price do these faithful gladiators pay? The cost to them is high, sad to say. The average NFL player is dead at 55, twenty years ahead of his non-athletic peers.

About 80% who go into the NFL married come out divorced.

About 50%, in spite of the incredible salaries earned, come out bankrupt.

The question perhaps is unanswerable, but needs to be asked nevertheless: is such a cost to family and self too great a price to pay for fleeting fame?

On the long train ride to Providence the next morning the article was very much on Ron's mind. It was the focus of attention as he and God had plenty of undisturbed time to reason together.

"God, what is it you really want for my life?" He prayed as he rode along. "Is this potential offer from Coach Anderson something you have for me, or is it a detour? I know that article in yesterday's 'paper was true: there are some crazy things that go on in pro football. But there are some legitimate, good people in pro football."

"Absolutely!" Came a resounding response to his spirit. "I have key people in all kinds of highly placed positions. And they are an honor to me. And they will continue to gain the praises of men because they have learned that those honors mean little. They have attained a success that lasts. They're not flattered by men. They have my peace and satisfaction within."

"Lord?" Ron asked his co-passenger. "Do you mean that I've been on this wild four-year rollercoaster just to learn a simple lesson that outward image is not important? But, Lord, I've known that. At least I've been trying to pattern my life that way."

"Yes, son," the reassuring voice spoke softly, "you've been learning well. However, success or prestige or honor in the eyes of men must be worn like a loose garment. You put it on. You take it off. Then you go on to the next thing.

"But you've allowed the whole desire for image in life to cling to you like a fine fitted suit. But, Ronny, status, in and of itself, is neither of importance nor of lasting significance."

The words had breathed softly on his spirit in love, but

they cut him to the quick like a sharp knife. Like a double edged sword.

He was humbled.

More significantly he was also set free, for the first time in his life, from the fear of failing.

"Lord," he repented, "I'm so sorry. Pro football is something I thought I had to have. I've not possessed it. It has possessed me.

"Thank you for being so patient with me. I now gladly release it all to you."

With that issue resolved he concentrated on the opportunity at Brown. After interviewing for the job he called his closest Christian friends and asked for counsel. One such friend whose opinion he valued greatly was one of his high school football coaches, Bob Tankard.

The response he received from all sources was firm and enthusiastic that he should go into coaching. He sensed from this that God indeed had been gently nudging him to enter football professionally. But as a coach, not as a player.

He was offered the job and accepted.

It was not his selected course, but it would keep him on the inside of the sport he loved, serving the Lord he had learned to love even more.

From his first day on the job at Brown, Ron realized that having knocked around four NFL training camps had not been a total washout. It had been good instruction. When he sat down with the rest of the staff for a planning session he was not a novice. He had rubbed elbows with some of the truly outstanding strategists of the game: men like Tom Landry, Mike Ditka, Raymond Berry and other great coaches. He had run in competition with guys like Walter Payton and Wesley Walker. He had been a good student of the game. Perhaps he could become a good teacher.

A few weeks before the start of practice that August Ron took advantage of a lull in his schedule for a vacation back in New York City. He wanted to have some parting hours with those who'd been such a support to him during his search for direction in life.

But again God had an unexpected blessing in store for him. Ron had first met Molvina Carter in January at a dinner party. He was instantly interested, for she was a very impressive woman. She had studied at Stanford, Oxford, and Columbia. Yet she was at the same time an extremely compassionate Christian. She had an unabashed love for those who are socially disadvantaged. To top it off she also was very attractive physically. She was pretty, wholesome, and had a shapely athletic stature developed from years of ballet and Caribbean-African dance.

Until he met Molvina relationships with women had been very discouraging. He had dated a few nice Christian gals, but he was impatient and restless: none lasted. He therefore had hesitated to try courting Molvina.

However, on his return to the city, the fascination of her inspired him to plunge ahead. He aggressively sought her company; and she complied. They discovered countless ways to share time together at church and with groups; but their favorite style of outing was for a quiet picnic in Central Park with lots of time to talk.

This woman was strong. She had a keen mind and insight for truth. There was a refreshing boldness and intensity for accuracy and attention to detail in her every endeavor. Yet it was accomplished with a powerful gift of compassion and loyalty, seasoned with a dash of shyness.

Ron saw Molvina's humility as her greatest quality. In the public, ego boosting profession of athletics which he was about to embark on, Molvina had a much needed and balancing devotion to privacy and excellence when no one else was looking. She desired neither praise nor recognition from the world. Just love and support from her Lord, family, and close friends.

Molvina Carter was a barrier to hypocrisy. No macho stuff or popularity seeking with this young lady. Ron Brown welcomed this special person in his heart. She was to become God's gift of balance in his life.

When summer ended and Ron returned to Rhode Island, he missed her and longed for her company. They maintained an intimate communication. No doubt about it, Ron Brown was falling in love. He had no intentions of ever losing her.

On recruiting trips to New York City Ron would visit Molvina at her aunts' home in Brooklyn, where she lived while attending graduate school. The two aunts, Dorothy and Jen, were not above trying a few matchmaking tricks.

One day Aunt Jen asked Ron to sit down with her for a very serious conversation. "Ron, could you make me one promise?" She requested solemnly.

His immediate response was, "Sure!" Knowing what the woman stood for as a believer and thinking of all that she had done for him made his answer spontaneous.

Then she laid it on him. "Will you love my niece Molvina forever?"

He knew the woman didn't just mean friendship. She was talking marriage. Big time.

Ron affirmed to her that he would always love her darling niece. He didn't know what course that promise might take, but it was the desire of his heart.

Just a month later Aunt Jen died suddenly.

Her life had been a great testimony to Christ. But the only real request she ever had made of Ron hit him again, square in the face, "Love Molvina forever!"

That in itself was easy. He had a powerful dose of love for her. He longed to share romantic moments with her daily for the rest of his life. He just hadn't contemplated marriage so soon. They'd only been dating for five months.

But why not? They loved each other. Definitely the flow of the current was moving in that direction. Ron prayed about it, sought some counsel, and proposed. To his delight and honor she accepted.

Romantically, they agreed that July 29, 1984, one year from the time of their first date, they would be joined by the Lord in marriage.

Having not met Molvina's family, Ron decided to

introduce himself to her parents by letter.

April 26, 1984

Dear Mr. and Mrs. Carter,

Let me start by saying that this is somewhat of a difficult letter to write because of the unique circumstances involved, yet a very pleasurable one as well, because of the great joy in my heart.

Molvina speaks fondly of you. From listening to her, and examining her life, I visualize you as strong Christians and consequently love-oriented. That's basically what I wanted to share with you in this letter: what God has done with love in my life.

As you've heard, I'm very much in love with your daughter. I know that the word gets tossed around often, but here God has intervened, tremendously. I met Molvina at a dinner party in January of 1983 in New York. Yes, I must admit I was instantly attracted to her—not love at first sight, but certainly `lots of like'. The dinner party contained `Stanfords' and `Princetons' and lots of `Ivy League' talk. I, myself, was trying very hard to concentrate on television.

It just so happened that on this particular evening the Super Bowl game was a little more interesting to me than Wall Street. However, I couldn't help overhearing Molvina's comments. I was extremely impressed that she was more people-oriented than money-oriented. Her stand inspired me to turn my attention away from the Super Bowl and to join forces with her in the discussion. When I left the apartment that night I was impressed with her. I bragged about her to my roommate for three days.

Relationships in my life had left a lot to be desired and I felt I could *never love again. However, God wouldn't let me give up. One day I was inspired to call Molvina. It seemed like a risk—but that risk turned out to be a gold mine for me. Little did we know that in less than a year we'd be talking about marrying each other.*

I'm traditional—and I'm asking for your blessing to marry your daughter, Molvina. I want you to approve of me.

I plan to love Molvina by giving my all to her—relinquishing my silly pride and ego—and rather cooperating and inspiring her to the fulfillment of her God-given talents. I know she'll do the same for me.

We believe God approves of our union. I hope you concur. My family certainly approves of Molvina. She is so special. I'm amazed at how much I love her.

Thank you so much for enduring this letter. It was emotional for me to write. I hope you've gotten a little better idea of who I am and what I'm all about.

I really am looking forward to meeting you and the family. May the LORD bless you. You have my love.

> *Sincerely,*
> *Ronald A. Brown*

Meanwhile Ron had directed the Brown frosh to a 1 and 5 season. Not an outstanding beginning to a coaching career. But freshmen play is regarded as an important proving ground, winning is not all important as it is with the varsity. Young guys, fresh out of high school, have an opportunity to mature in competition with a select group of their peers. Neither the press nor the electronic media give much concern to that level of play; but it is just as significant to collegiate football as farm teams are to professional baseball.

In addition to the satisfaction of being intimately involved with some dedicated young athletes and the camaraderie of the coaching staff, Ron loved the challenge of academics at that great institution. Being an alumnus also afforded him ready recognition on campus. He was remembered not only for his football and academic achievements, but he was well remembered for the clean image he had left behind. (Since he had never allowed anyone to see inside him, no one had the same low opinion which he had held against himself; and against which he had struggled so long.) He was respected. Notably so.

Though coaching, training, and recruiting players was the profession which began to unfold before him, his primary purpose was to be God's man, a witness. Whether one-on-one with a troubled student or in group Bible studies, he began to carve a niche for himself in the spiritual fiber of the campus.

At last he also learned what had happened to Harry Walls. On a recruiting trip he got into conversation with another Christian coach. As he shared his testimony and gave credit to Harry's input into his life, he lamented that he didn't know what had become of the man.

"Oh, yes," the other coach declared, "I knew Harry. You know, he went to Brown University for only one purpose. He wanted to get a Bible study started on the football team. Once that was established, he transferred to a divinity school somewhere to become a pastor."

Although 1983 could be qualified as a good testing time for the freshman team, the season was a disaster for the varsity Brown Bruins. Even for a school which prides itself principally on being an academic institution, a 4 and 5 record was unthinkable. Consequently, with pressure from alumni, fans, and disgruntled students, the entire football coaching staff was fired. The sacking included the freshman staff as well, which spelled an apparent early doom to Ron's new found career.

A few days after the house cleaning Ron was home on the island with his parents.

"Son, what are you goin' to do now?" His father asked with concern. "Everything seemed to be going so well for you."

"I don't know, Dad," Ron answered "This decision was sudden, but not really unexpected. I mean coaching is a tough profession. Coaches have to produce. The staff just didn't put up the right won-loss record.

"At this point I have no idea what to do next. I was really beginning to enjoy the job. I thought this was God's plan for me! And then boom!"

"But why did they fire you? I can see why they got rid of the head coach. But why you?" His dad questioned.

"That's the way it works, Dad," Ron explained flatly. "You see, he had the say as to who he wanted on his staff. So when he goes we all go. That way when a new coach is hired he's free to choose a staff to his liking.

"This way there was a total clean sweep."

Though he tried to act low key about it with his folks, Ron was in turmoil about the sudden shift in job security for a reason other than what it meant to him. His relationship with Molvina had progressed steadily. They were together at every opportunity and planned to make it permanent. The date was firm for a wedding at her home in San Diego. How could he go through with the responsibilities of marriage and be on the streets looking for work at the same time?

Ron returned to campus the next day just as the news broke publicly. The trustees had wasted no time in selecting a new head coach. John Rosenberg, former defensive backfield coach at Penn State and with the USFL's Philadelphia Stars, was hired and hit town in full stride. Though Brown University has no spring football program, Rosenberg had a lot of work to do in order to build a staff and get them involved in his new system. One of his first orders of business was to contact Ron and ask him to come to his office. After a brief greeting and introduction he got right to the matter at hand.

He put Ron to an on the spot test of his knowledge of

football. He was aware that in addition to being head freshman coach Ron had assisted the varsity defensive back coach. "Ron step up to the chalkboard and diagram a few defensive back techniques and coverages for me."

Without questioning as to why, Ron took chalk in hand and explained in detail five or six defensive coverages and the individual techniques associated with them.

Rosenberg listened attentively. After Ron had run through schemes for fifteen minutes the coach interrupted him, "Thanks, Ron. Sit down over here and let's talk.

"Ron, I've heard a lot about you for years. You had quite an impact on the Ivy League as a player. But more importantly, now, you did a great job with the freshmen players this last year, inspite of the 1 and 5 record. However, I think Anderson made a mistake in putting you in that spot."

Ron gulped. The ax was about to fall.

"You have a great potential in coaching," Rosenberg continued. "I'd like for you to consider moving up to the varsity as defensive back coach.

"How about it?"

Ron was shocked by the offer. He wasn't being fired. He was being promoted. And into an area of specific expertise. He was amazed at the sudden turn of events, yet he smiled inwardly as he realized who had opened up this expanded opportunity for him. God was in charge. This was the Lord's stamp of approval on coaching as a career for him.

It seemed that a whole lifetime flashed before his eyes as he saw God leading him into the future, but his instant response to the offer was, "Yes, Sir! I can handle that."

And handle it he did. Within two years the media dubbed the defensive backfield for the Bruins as "The Wreckin' Crew". This was accomplished in spite of an off and on conflict within the coaching staff against the head coach. Even Ron was frequently at odds with Rosenberg over strategy and principles, though they maintained a good working relationship.

Meanwhile Ron gained the stabilizing support of a strong

Christian wife. He and Molvina tied the knot just as they had planned. No longer did he have to look around for a confirming opinion (or contrary advice) on key issues. Molvina was always there, although low key, with encouragement or challenge.

Ron's fourth year at Brown was a difficult one. Recurring problems with the head coach were too much for both players and assistant coaches. Some left. Hank Small shifted to Lehigh as head football coach. Mike Church went to the University of Texas-El Paso, as defensive coordinator. Ron also had a job offer from Hank Small at Lehigh. Yet he held steady.

The coaching staff that remained was in continuing turmoil over a key decision by Rosenberg to not give John Townsend the assignment as defensive coordinator. JT had been in college football for many years at several major Division I schools. He and Ron not only shared coaching similarities, but because both were black they were united in some common life issues as well. Rosenberg devised a unique plan to rotate his defensive assistants to coordinate the defense on a game by game basis. The decision was an obvious hindrance to continuity. It strained many relationships, even between Ron and JT. Eventually though they were able to reaffirm their friendship stronger than ever.

God also gave Ron a new ally in the Christian outreach on campus. Biff Poggi came on board as an assistant coach. In short order the two men became great friends. Together they organized a Bible study for all coaches at the University. Later, after Poggi had moved on to a coaching job in Baltimore, they shared their individual dreams with each other for helping underprivileged kids. They realized that they had one and the same vision. So they teamed up to start an "I CAN" camp, first in South Carolina, and later in Nebraska.

In all the busy involvement as a coach, with its heavy schedule of travel for recruiting and being constantly on call for every need of athletes, Ron maintained one thing as more important: his relationship with God came first.

He abandoned forever the ego need of building an image for himself. He knew that God's main purpose for him was to use athletics as a platform from which to share the truth of Christ.

Chapter 12
REALITY BEYOND THE DREAM

• •

Ron Brown had dreamed big from the first time he donned a pair of sneakers and got into athletics. He wanted more than anything to be right smack dab in the middle of professional sports. It was the apparent, right thing for him to do. He wasn't kidding himself. He had some basic talents. He could go far.

And, it was not just a case of youthful ego on his part. He received continuous reinforcing encouragement along the way from a host of people. His coaches goaded him toward perfect performance. His parents watched adoringly from the sidelines. Whatever it was he secretly lacked in inner confidence others made up for with unbridled support. For instance, when he was only beginning to develop his physical skills and was an unproven quantity, his basketball coach at Martha's Vineyard helped him gain a vision of the future. Jay Schofield drilled him consistently not only in fundamentals of basketball but in the basics of life also, hitting hard on academic and social development. Schofield kept feeding the youngster with enthusiasm for stretching beyond, to dream. And then to dream again.

Yet for balance there was Gerry Gerolamo, the high school's head football coach. He wisely added the challenge for Ron to remain humble in the light of what Gerolamo was certain would be success.

Years later when Ron returned home after being cut by the Dallas Cowboys another former coach, a strong born again Christian, Bob Tankard, came right over to see him. "Now, Ronny," he said firmly, somewhat fatherly, "I know you're feeling down. Who wouldn't? You had a great chance and it was just snatched away from you!

"But, Ronny, that's not the end. Sure Dallas is big time. But so are the 49ers, the Bears, the Broncos, and the Patriots."

"Sure, there are other teams in the NFL," Ron moaned, "but who's goin' to give a second chance to a reject."

"You're not a reject, Man!" Tankard, affirmed. "Let's get that shoulder back in shape and try again.

"You can do it!"

With such affirmation continually coming his way Ron pressed persistently on with his dream. Certainly if it had not been for Christ's transforming influence he would've fallen by the wayside. Jesus was the one who made the significant difference. He put others in Ron's life to further strengthen him in his pursuit as they often supplied the confidence when he had little or none.

Naturally Ron met other disappointed dreamers along the way. Unfulfilled in theirs hopes they all seemed to have two basic things in common: at least a bit of talent and a driving desire to be famous. Some wanted the glory of limelight success in sports so badly that they lost view of anything and everything else. There was no balance in their lives.

One such man left a lasting, tragic impression on Ron. He first met Jim Tressler on the coaching staff at Brown.

When the whole staff was fired the following year, Tressler's bubble burst. He had dreamed, but it was greatly exaggerated, and he had no follow through of his own. He slid from the pinnacle and faded away. With no further goal or plan, Jim drifted back to his old hometown in Ohio to sell cars. Disillusioned. Purposeless. Frustrated.

He was only in his mid-forties, with a wonderful wife, and two daughters in college. One day, while all alone and depressed, convinced that no one cared, he shot himself.

The newspaper account was a shock. Ron wept as he read the news aloud to Molvina at the breakfast table. He laid the newspaper aside silently, and thought deeply as he slowly regained his composure. How gracious God had been in giving him a purpose far beyond this world's fame for which to live.

Unfortunately the death of this one fine man was not an isolated incident.

Tragedy struck again. Another coaching acquaintance, later at the University of Nebraska, also committed suicide.

Ron sorrowed because of the loss of such energetic men, at the prime of life. "But," he observed to Molvina after the second coach's funeral, "don't we also have a bit of these men in us. If it weren't for God being in control of our lives, we'd be just as prone to disaster. The way these guys died was tragic. But the reason they died is worse. They died for want of a reputation in the eyes of the world, feeling they had fallen short of success.

"I remember the feeling," he admitted quietly.

"But how thankful I am that God kept the dream alive in me until I was able to get beyond it to the reality he has for me—us."

Molvina did not reply. The truth was too solemn.

"You know," Ron continued momentarily, "a Christian friend came up to me my first year back at Brown as a coach and said, 'This isn't so bad, Ron. At least you got God's second best.'"

"A friend, you say," Molvina sarcastically reacted.

Ron smiled at her unguarded support. "At least God was able to use his comment to my benefit. I gave a lot of thought to what he said. Had I been forced to settle for God's second best? The more I thought about it the more I knew he was wrong, the more satisfied I became of what God was doing in my life. The Lord showed me that the whole definition of success that I'd been geared to, even after I became a Christian, was still flawed with outward emphasis. Looking always for image.

"I found that the real answer is only in the Word of God. This is our playbook," Ron continued as he reached for his Bible on a nearby stand, "showing us through obedience, his formula for lasting satisfaction. The Lord explained it perfectly to the children of Israel in Joshua 1:8-9." He turned the pages to the passage and read aloud:

> Do not let this Book of the Law depart from your mouth; meditate on it day and night, so that you may be careful to do everything written in it. Then you will be prosperous and successful. Have I not commanded you? Be strong and courageous. Do not be terrified; do not be discouraged, for the Lord your God will be with you wherever you go.

"Now, I've gained a different dream, a higher goal. I just want to please Jesus Christ."

"I agree," Molvina affirmed. "It seems to me that God designed all along for you to be a coach. He simply used the so-called failures in pro football as your training ground.

"Like young David, running from Saul for years before God raised him to be king as he had promised.

"Or like Paul, spending three years in the desert before exploding on the scene for a worldwide ministry."

A short time after that, Ron sat in his car one day praying before going to work at Brown University. He began to talk to God about his future in coaching. He was feeling apprehensive. "I'm at a small Ivy League school—the least experienced coach on the staff. Is there a future for a black coach? Will people ever feel comfortable about hiring black head football coaches? Is it always going to be such a struggle?"

He prayed for wisdom.

God responded quietly with assurance to Ron's heart, "Don't seek anything first—except conforming to Christ. Don't wait to become a head coach before you start having an impact on people spiritually. Start now. Go hard. Use my gifts now—even as an assistant coach to bring glory to me.

"I'll handle the promotions. Trust in Matthew 6:33 and Psalm 75. Just be faithful."

Ron did move forward in his witness, inspired greatly by Les Steckel, an assistant coach with the nearby Patriots at the time. They talked extensively from time to time and became good friends. Ron watched the man stand true to God while going through much tribulation as a coach. Steckel kept his eyes always on Christ, which served also as an inspiring boost to Ron in regard to coaching.

Ron and Molvina enjoyed the four seasons at his alma mater. It was an important proving ground for Ron in his God-ordained profession. But it was time, he considered, to move on. He began testing the waters. He interviewed first at Baylor with head football coach, Grant Taeff, who also had a powerful Christian witness. Taeff eventually decided to hire someone else. But he appreciated Ron's talent so much that he promised to recommend him for another position elsewhere.

That vow was shortly fulfilled.

Tom Osborne, head football coach at the University of Nebraska, heard about Ron from Mike Church who had coached with Ron at Brown University and who was then defensive coordinator at the University of Texas-El Paso. Osborne called Ron to get acquainted.

Ron promptly called Taeff, at seven o'clock the next morning, and asked him to speak to Osborne on his behalf.

Taeff did so.

Osborne invited Ron to Lincoln for an interview, after which he narrowed the field down to Brown and one other.

Ron and Molvina prayed about the opportunity and were in agreement to accept the job of receivers coach for the Cornhuskers if it was offered.

Osborne decided on Brown.

With a Big Eight, Division I school like Nebraska, spring football is an invaluable training time. So Ron and Molvina made a quick transfer from Providence to Lincoln in order to be on the job for the April sessions.

As the Huskers' receivers coach Ron knew from the first day of practice at Nebraska that he was into a much higher caliber of college football. The media attention directed toward him as an assistant coach for the Big Red was more intense than anything Ron had experienced at Brown. The press back in Rhode Island had never cared so much. Ron realized right off that "fish bowl" living would be at its highest in the football crazed state of Nebraska.

Ron dove into the challenge of working under the direction of Tom Osborne with excitement. It was an outstanding opportunity to learn through the tutelage of one of the most respected college football coaches of the last quarter century.

He envisioned also that he could make an impact in the realm of race relations. After a decline in the 1970s, racial incidents on college campuses had begun to increase dramatically during the 1980s. The often quoted words of Gladstone, "All it takes for evil to prevail is for good men to do nothing," were etched deep into his character. Ron was committed to making a difference.

"I'd like to raise the level of consciousness of whites, blacks, everyone, and remove the ignorance," he told an Omaha sports reporter. "Racism, subtle or overt, hurts not only minority-race people. It diminishes us all.

"God created men and women of all colors equal. They ought to be looked at for the content of their character, not the color of their skin. We have to defeat the stereotypes."

Another dream Ron had nurtured for years and which he took along to Nebraska was his desire to continue to minister meaningfully to underprivileged kids. He had been involved in such outreach from his early days as a Christian while in New York City. This vision to do something lasting wouldn't go away.

One day, back in New York, while in graduate school, he had knelt in prayer and sought God's leadership in four specifics which were most important to him. He still had a yearning to make it as a pro football player; but having missed his first opportunities he knew the prospect was dim.

He also was experiencing a sense of loneliness since the relationship with Audrey had faded into oblivion. "Lord!" He pleaded, tears welling up in his eyes, "I trust you to bring the woman of your choosing into my life. I want someone I can give myself to in a united effort to bring glory to you."

As he continued in his prayer session, Ron concentrated on what had become a burning passion. "Father, I really want to be able to do something to help underprivileged kids. I don't know exactly what you have for me next, but I do know it's not to be a hospital administrator. Oh! I'm going to finish this master's degree. But, that's not for me. I just ask that whatever else you have for me, please use me for the sake of kids.

"And," he concluded with a dream from his youth, "I want to be a positive role model. There are so many injustices in society. I promise you that every chance you give me to be heard, I will give Jesus Christ all the credit for any success I have."

Within three years God had responded to all but one of Ron's petitions. Pro football was a qualified no: coaching was the answer. Loneliness had been washed away: he and Molvina were matched in love. And a high profile platform from which to be heard was a reality.

There had been countless opportunities to help individual kids, yet Ron was restless for something more. He devised a plan to search out possibilities in the south. While coaching at Brown he realized that schools of the Ivy League didn't frequent the south to recruit. Ron convinced Coach Rosenberg that there was a gold mine of potential talent down there for Brown University.

On a ten day swing through the southeastern states, Ron searched out athletes and also gained invaluable coaching clues by observing spring practices at major universities. But his side agenda was to see first hand the poverty and inequalities of life in remote rural areas. In one town after another he walked through the streets and visited with young and old alike.

As he headed back to Providence a vision began to form, a plan to bring disadvantaged kids together for a few hours each day for a week. Sports would be a main feature, but a challenge to excellence in all areas of endeavor would be the focus.

That vision became reality as well when he and Biff Poggi got their first "I CAN" summer camp underway in 1987 in Beaufort, South Carolina. With the help of the local chapter of the Boy's Club, children between the ages of ten and fifteen were carefully selected from neighborhoods throughout the area to ensure a broad mix of racial and social backgrounds. The idea being to break down the insidious barriers that even divide kids.

Ron and Biff wanted a way of combining the best in athletics and academics, while at the same time transforming attitudes. Since most underprivileged kids have experienced a negative view of life, living under a dark shadow of doubt both about themselves and their opportunities, an understandable response to challenge often is, "I Can't!"

Ron and Biff came up with the positive strategy of "I CAN!" An acronym for Ideal of Christian Athademitudes in the Neighborhood.

"There is no such word as 'athademitudes'," Biff challenged when Ron first coined the word.

"There is now," Ron laughed. "Look! It puts into one expression everything we want to accomplish with the kids: athletics, academics, and attitudes. And we want them to understand that with the right attitude they can accomplish anything."

So, in addition to his optimism for a meaningful career of coaching at a football powerhouse, like Nebraska, Ron knew that God had other purposes for him. Surely an ever expanding "I CAN" also was transplanted with him to the lands along the Platte.

Chapter 13
THE
SURPRISE
DECISION

• •

Working throughout the off season as a recruiter for the Nebraska football program is equivalent to a full-time job in itself. Yet Ron savored every bit of it. He loved the challenge of building rapport one-on-one. Compared to the Ivy League from which he came, the Big Eight search for talent is intense and aggressive. Days on the road and in the air were long, exhausting, and extensive. But such effort brought Ron face to face with some of the finest high school and junior college athletes in the nation. It had been in his first such recruiting year at Nebraska that Ron came into contact with Victor Stachmus, built a friendship, and won the struggle for the gifted young man's commitment to play football for the Big Red: and was there to help him into Christ's wheelbarrow of faith.

In addition to Victor, 1987 produced a bumper crop of young men for Nebraska as other future standout players signed on the dotted line. There were guys like Lance Lewis, Mike Grant, Bruce Pickens, William Washington, Tyrone Hughes, and Jon Bostick. The Cornhusker staff had done a great job.

Ron, however, had little time to rejoice with the rest of the coaching staff as that signing season ended. He was organizing his plans for spring practice when word came of his father's unexpected death on April 9, 1988. Ironically, Victor Stachmus was diagnosed with leukemia just one week later. It proved to be a tough spring.

Ron and his father had quietly enjoyed a very close, meaningful relationship between themselves. That was quite an accomplishment for two men who for years found difficulty in expressing themselves emotionally. Though the bond between them was basically unspoken, it was at the same time unbreakable. The son always knew that his dad was there for him, and the father had impeccable trust in the boy. They liked each other and enjoyed being together. They just didn't find words to talk much about it.

During Ron's last year on the staff at Brown University his dad asked if they could make a trip together in the summer of '86. "Ronny, let's go south—to see the new south. I haven't been down there since I was in the army during World War II. Even though I had a uniform on, I had to go to the back of the bus—in America no less. I would love to see how much things have changed—maybe even ride in the front of a bus—just for the fun of it."

"Sure, Dad! That would be great. I can take a couple weeks off this summer. You and I can have a great trip."

They made plans. Ron eagerly anticipated the time alone with his dad. But when the time came for them to leave, the southern tier of states was gripped in a terrific heat wave. His long years of hard work had taken their toll on Arthur Brown—he couldn't stand hot weather. They had to cancel the trip. Instead they sensibly stayed home in the relatively cool comfort of Martha's Vineyard.

It was a preordained time. Ron had yearned for years to have an uninterrupted time to talk to his dad about Jesus, just as he had with hundreds of others. In contrast, his mom was easy to talk to about spiritual matters: she had been converted in her own living room one night after watching Billy Graham on television. But his dad had maintained a respectable distance in spiritual matters. He always had been a devout, religious man. He'd gone to church all his life and saw to it that his kids did too. But he kept talk about God to a minimum.

One evening, as the two of them sat on the front porch, the conversation flowed naturally into the subject which was of greatest importance to Ron: Jesus Christ and what God had accomplished in him and for him personally.

"Ronny," his dad confessed openly, "I've been around this earth for 68 years and I've never had that kind of satisfaction you talk about. I've worked hard and no one has ever given me anything.

"Now, I'm not complainin' about the work. I think that's how it's supposed to be. But I've been put down and closed out of opportunities that white folk take for granted, and just because I'm black. I think that's mighty unfair.

"I think your mom and you and your sister would'a' had it a whole lot easier if we'd not been born black."

Ron looked at his dad in amazement. The man had stood as a sentinel of cool understanding throughout the years of unfair racism and had kept his counsel to himself. Never had he insinuated any bitterness in his soul. Bitterness, not that he was black—he was proud of that; but anger because society made that into a critical barrier.

"Dad," Ron said with spiritual insight, "you know, no one who comes into this world can determine how they're going to be born. But! God does give us the option to be born again—to start a new life in Jesus Christ."

His dad looked at him intently. Listening.

Ron continued, "Dad, it really begins at the point of our recognizing our need for something more. We look at our mistakes—our sins—our anger, then we turn to God for an answer.

"1 John 1:9 says:
'If we confess our sins, he is faithful and just and will
forgive us our sins and purify us from all unrighteousness.'

"And we all need forgiveness—you, me, mom, everyone who ever lived—except Jesus.

"That's what Paul meant when he wrote in Romans 3:23:

'For all have sinned and fall short of the glory of God.'

"But then he adds the promise in Romans 6:23:

'The wages of sin is death, but the gift of God is eternal life through Jesus Christ our Lord.'

"Dad, Jesus Christ accomplished all that for us when he died on the cross. He died that we might be forgiven and begin to live for him."

"Ronny," his dad interrupted, "I believe this and would love to. I'm just not sure that I can."

"Dad, you can!" Ron insisted, and without pausing for breath plunged ahead boldly, "would you like to pray right now and ask Jesus to come into your life as your Lord and Savior?"

His father looked at him admiringly, knowing that his son had given him the words that he himself should have taught his son many years before. His voice, however, did not quaver as he replied, "Yes, son, I would."

As the two of them sat praying in the cool of the evening, Ron was overwhelmed with gratitude to God for this rare opportunity with his dad.

With firm voice Arthur Brown poured out the burden of his heart to God in repentance and acceptance. Silence punctuated his conclusion. Tears welled up in his eyes as he declared in simple appreciation, "Thank you, Ronny. Thank you, Ronny."

Less than two years later, as he took that sudden break in spring training to be with his mother and sister, Ron wrote in epitaph of his father:

My Dad had a great ability to see potential in someone—and make that person feel good about himself.

Here's a man who by the world's standards was not highly educated, nor influential in the public forum. Yet he was wiser than many because he knew how to communicate easily with people from ages two to ninety-two. I never saw him uncomfortable around people. He could make you laugh or he could be stern and command attention, whatever it took to get his wisdom across.

His most admirable quality was his love and commitment to his wife, my mom. He treated her with such great respect. All the little things. He was home every night, and even though he worked during the day, his heart was always home. His relationship with my mom was extremely inspirational to me and my wife.

Back in 1957 he and my mom decided to adopt a child from a foundling home in New York City. That was me, and two years later my parents went back to the same place to adopt my sister Theresa. It was so natural for that man and his wife to love, no matter if you were miles away. They knew love and commitment, and exemplified it.

I am so blessed because I still am a recipient of that love even after his death.

The greatest memory I have of my Dad came just two years ago, in the summer of 1986. We were sitting on the porch and began to talk about life in a very serious way. He shared with me his 68 years of ups and downs. He realized that life was more than paying bills, going to work and wishing the best for his wife and children. We talked about God and although he spent most of his life going to church on a regular basis, he realized that he had never personally made Jesus Christ the center of his life. The next thing we knew, for the first time ever, we were actually praying together. And he asked Christ to be the center of his life. I treasure that day with all my heart.

His favorite jazz musician was Jimmy Smith. He often played a song from one of Smith's albums named "I'll Close My Eyes". On April 9, 1988 Arthur Brown closed his eyes for the last time here on earth. However, at the instant of death, he opened his eyes to a new life— eternity with the Lord. I love my dad. I miss him. Yet he's preserved for a future date when we will reunite.

With the death of the man who meant more to him than any other, and then on the heels of that the death of the recruit who was so close to his heart, Ron was all the more determined to share the message of Jesus Christ with all who would listen—especially his players. He wanted them to know success. The kind of achievement that you don't have to be a winner to obtain. The style of status that keeps you feelin' good even when the goin' is rough.

Being introduced as the receivers coach for the University of Nebraska sounds impressive in itself, but loyal fans of the team sometimes chuckle. Head coach Tom Osborne believes in running the ball, running the ball, running the ball. The Cornhusker pass receivers and their coach often are like the proverbial Maytag repairman, the loneliest man in town.

Yet Ron Brown is one who, from his first day, never laughed at the task. He knew that receivers have another significant function. They don't just stand around on the gridiron waiting for a pass to come their way, once in a lifetime. Receivers must also block well if a running game is to work at all. Much to the credit of the blocking prowess of the receivers, the Nebraska Cornhuskers lead the nation in rushing yardage.

Ron also determined from the beginning of his tenure in Lincoln that if Coach Osborne called for only one pass in a game, he intended for his man to catch the ball. He drilled his tight ends, wing backs, and split ends to high proficiency. They responded to the challenge and in 1989 Nebraska finished in the top ten in the United States in touchdown passes caught; and tied the Big Eight record for most touchdown passes thrown in a season. Not only so, but the Husker receivers also had one of the highest yards per catch averages (18.8 yards) in the nation.

In Ron Brown's South Stadium office in Lincoln, are training video tapes on receiving, all the information any young man needs to know in learning to catch a football. Yet failure can be summed up easily. In it all, there are basically three reasons why a person drops a ball that's within reach.

Number one. The receiver goes out on his pass pattern, turns around, and sees the ball coming just six inches away. He has a bead on the ball. All he has to do is take it. Suddenly, however, a thought runs through his mind, "Humh, when I catch this ball I'm goin' to make a move on this defender like he's never seen before. I'm goin' to spin away from him. I'm goin' to start wrigglin' and streakin' down the sideline, avoid some other tacklers, score a touchdown, the fans are goin' to go crazy, my name's in the newspaper, my face is on TV. It's goin' to be great!"

All of that thought process takes just a split second while the ball is still approaching those yearning hands; and he takes his eyes off the ball to head downfield; and it drops to the ground.

Never take your eyes off the ball. It's the first lesson!

But, that in itself doesn't necessarily spell success for a receiver. On the Cornhusker practice field it sometimes sounds like an incantation as Coach Brown reminds his charges over and over, "Watch the ball in! Look the ball in. All the way in."

Dutifully, ironically, young men stare at the pigskin as it hits them in the helmet or flops off their fingertips.

That underscores the second reason for failure to catch a well thrown pass: lack of concentration. A man may be looking at the ball but his mind is not on the ball. He's thinking about a bad grade he got from a tough professor, or a misunderstanding with a girl that made him mad, or on the "silly" passing drill itself.

All kinds of things can race through a person's mind if his real intent is not on the matter at hand: catching the ball.

The third reason why some players drop the ball was evident in the Cornhusker's 1988 game at UCLA. Dana Brinson, all spry 160 pounds of him, leaped up and stretched out to grab a pass. Just as the ball hit his fingertips he was smashed hard by a UCLA linebacker. Dana was knocked out cold. He caught the ball, but he lay on the ground for a long time.

Fans cheered as he eventually got to his feet, but the unexpressed question was, "After a hit like that, will that boy ever overcome fear when another pass comes his way."

For a lot of players, when they come racing across the

field, even though there is no one else around, because he's been through the frightening experience of being flattened by a bruising tackle, there is fear and those hands don't go up with the same authority. And the ball slides off the fingers.

Such was not the case with Dana Brinson. Not only did he finish the UCLA game, but he played the rest of the season with a neck collar and was drafted by the San Diego Chargers.

In sharing Christ with one of his players one morning, Ron reminded him of the three reasons why passes fall incomplete. "That's why for the first twenty-two years of my life I couldn't catch on to God's plan." He admitted.

"God is like the quarterback, getting ready to throw the ball. The ball is in the form of his Son, Jesus Christ.

"I didn't have my eyes on Jesus. I had my eyes on the world. I wanted popularity. I wanted to please people. I couldn't accept Christ. I wasn't looking his way.

"In college I began to understand something about Jesus Christ because people were talking about him; but my mind wasn't on him. My mind was on the success of fulfilling other's expectations. My priorities were different. Jesus was way down the list. Even though I believed in him I wasn't making him number one in my life. I was dropping the ball because my full concentration wasn't on him.

"Also, there was the fear. The fear of failure. The fear of wondering if my life was such a miserable mess, how could I honor God. The fear of what my buddies would think if I became a "God Squad member".

"But God is very merciful. God sent me two receivers coaches, a guy named Harry and a gal named Audrey. They weren't the answer in my life. God is the answer. But he used them to help me see him. To help me, by the example of their lives, to have courage to reach out and make the most important catch of my life—Jesus Christ.

"I want to encourage you too. God is throwing you a pass. If you haven't made Jesus Christ your Lord and Savior. If you haven't made that great catch. I encourage you to do that.

Reach out with your heart and make the greatest catch of your life.

"There is no greater joy than that. I have no regrets. I would never turn back."

"Thanks, Coach," the young player nodded in agreement. He too wanted to get on God's team—as a starter.

In his first three seasons on the coaching staff at Nebraska Ron assisted in helping the Cornhuskers roll up an impressive record of 31 wins against only 6 losses. And, as had been the pattern for years, the Big Red went on to three consecutive post season bowl appearances.

Early in the 1989 campaign several of the recurring powerhouses in college football had disappointing losses. The national press was looking for someone to tag number one in the country. Nebraska, though a young team, had surprised everyone with early, lopsided victories. In contrast to other perennial favorites which stumbled coming out of the starting gate, the Cornhuskers performed well under the field leadership of senior-first-year-starting quarterback Gerry Gdowski.

Then came the Colorado game. Hype was high. Sportsmen used that often overused phrase "game of the decade". It was plain to see that the winner would be heralded as number one.

Unbelievably, on the first play from scrimmage, Tom Osborne—the run, run, run coach—called for a pass. Within seconds the deft hands of Bryan Carpenter reached out for the ball, pulled it to his chest, and raced into the end zone.

Flash: Nebraska 7, Colorado 0.

The fans who had traveled to Boulder, joined by thousands in front of their television screens, rocked with enthusiasm.

However, college football is composed of four equal quarters. The team ahead at the end wins. Final score: Colorado 27, Nebraska 21.

For some "die hard" Nebraska fans it was the end of the season. For them a loss to Colorado or Oklahoma is a "wipeout".

Fortunately college coaches and athletes cannot key in on just one game. Those who are at the task full time know that one game does not make a season. Their eyes are just as much on continuity and progress as on the won or loss column. They don't have the luxury of brooding over defeats or gloating over victories.

At three o'clock sharp the next afternoon the Cornhusker coaches were back at work, preparing themselves for the next battle. Though another trip to the Orange Bowl undoubtedly was lost along with the Colorado game, it was not the end of the season. There were skills to be refined.

But, besides heading back constantly to the drawing board, well disciplined coaches also build variety into their lives. Ron Brown is in demand continually as a speaker. Immediately after the Kansas State game in 1989, for instance, as soon as he completed his responsibilities with the team and homecoming alumni, he rushed out to the nearby Lincoln Correctional Center to share the message of Christ in his life with a fellowship of inmates. All as a part of his promise to God to honor him in everything.

At about that same time Ron had an unexpected challenge cross his path. Along with some others in the coaching fraternity, he had been aware for months that there were problems within the football program back at Brown University. However, he had no idea that he would be singled out as a leading prospect for the head job.

At first he kept the news to himself. He and Molvina talked it through. There were many uncertainties about making a move. They were well settled in their home and happily had established a broad base of relationships. Equally important, the opportunities for ministry within the state and beyond, had provided Ron a solid evangelical platform for Jesus Christ. He was well known in his stance of openly proclaiming the truth of Christ, insisting on an end to racial bigotry, and seeking assistance for orphans and the underprivileged. Also, the "I CAN" program was going well with a third camp on line to begin in northern Nebraska among Native American children.

Though all of those circumstances were important considerations, Ron nevertheless was a football coach and going to Brown University could be a significant career move. He talked to many football people for their general opinions. But he strongly considered the advice of a few trusted friends and sought their prayer support.

Ron swallowed hard one morning as he stepped out of his office in the South Stadium. It was time to talk to the one man in Lincoln he respected most in regard to football and whom he also held in high admiration as a Christian. Tom Osborne had brought him to Lincoln and introduced him to the power football of the Big Eight. They had become good friends. Nonetheless, Ron was nervous. He didn't want to appear to be an opportunist.

"Coach," he began after they had settled down in high— backed chairs in Osborne's office, "I think you should be one of the first to know that I've been approached by Brown University in regard to the head coach's job there. At this point, they have several people they're considering. Certainly the job isn't mine for the asking. But I didn't want you to hear a rumor about it from someone else."

"I appreciate that, Ron," Coach Osborne replied in his own inimitable, unruffled way. "But, I must say I'm not surprised."

An expression of shock registered on Ron's face.

"Oh, certainly I didn't know about Brown University's approach," Tom continued. "I just mean, I believe that a man of your ability is always going to be sought after as a coach."

"I just don't want you to think that I'm using you and the University of Nebraska as a stepping stone—especially since I just came here from Brown three years ago," Ron explained.

"No, don't worry about that," Osborne assured him. "I know you better than that. I'd certainly hate to lose your talents, but this could be a great opportunity for you. Do they want to interview you?"

"I told them I couldn't come for an interview until after Thanksgiving—after the season's over but before we begin practice for the Fiesta Bowl," Ron explained.

"You have my support, Ron, whether you stay or go. Be sure to keep me posted though," Osborne advised.

The unhurried meditation and search for an answer then came to an abrupt halt. Before Ron and Molvina could thoroughly sort through their own thoughts on the matter the news broke across the campus and in the press. Immediately they were inundated with perhaps well-meaning, but unsolicited, advice from every corner. Being the football mecca that it is, Nebraska is not short of "experts" on every facet of the game. Many offered an opinion.

Ron, however, had acquired one immeasurable asset in decision making. Prayer had become for him not an empty ritual performance but a time of personal communion with God. Through patient reflection and waiting he had learned to lay matters before his Heavenly Father; and then trust in the resulting leadership.

This dependence upon God was truly important in the face of conflicting conclusions from two individuals whose opinion he valued greatly: his mother and one high school coach.

When Coach Tankard learned that Ron was in consideration for the top job at Brown he was elated and enthused. He had no doubts on the matter. He told Pearl Brown, "Absolutely, Ron, should take the job! Why here he's only thirty-three years old and can step into leadership at one of the most respected institutions in the Ivy League.

"Not only that. He would also be the first black head football coach in the history of the league—as well as one of just a few in America today. It would be a great step for advancing not only himself but society too.

"And this is a rebuilding time at Brown. He can put his own individual stamp on the program.

"With God's help—and a few successful years at his alma mater—Division I schools will be beating a path to his door."

Ron of course was flattered, though not surprised, by Tankard's endorsement. From their first association in high school, the coach always had unconditional support for him.

On the other hand, Ron was totally astonished by the response of his mother. He had assumed that she would be excited about him returning east, so near to home—especially because of the recent loss of her husband and her own advancing years. However, there was no selfishness in her opinion. She too was adamant, "Ronny, why would you even think of leaving Nebraska? God has been so good to you there. You have everything a young man could want: a great wife, a fine home, a job you like, respect in the community.

"No, son! I don't think you should go back to Brown!"

When the possibility of being head coach for the Bruins first presented itself Ron was one of many applicants. He flew east to interview for the position in November. By early December the list had been pared to four. Ron was a leading candidate. But he was also informed that a "small number of alumni" were not in favor of being the first in the league to hire a black head coach. They didn't want to set a precedent. Nonetheless, the university officials were made of sterner stuff. On Christmas Eve, Ron was told that the job was his if he wanted it. He sought to postpone a final decision until after the Cornhusker's Fiesta Bowl contest, but the officials at Brown, understandably wanted to put an end to speculations. They set December 30 as a deadline for his answer.

Not only did Brown University need an answer, but it seemed that everyone in Nebraska wanted the inside scoop as well. Big Red fans take their football seriously—it's the tail that wags the dog in Nebraska. Consequently, while trying to concentrate on his responsibilities to the team, Ron was beset on every hand. The telephone in his room at the Fiesta Bowl site was constantly ringing—inquiring minds wanting to know. His players were nagged continually by reporters trying to get an inside exclusive as to what Ron was going to do. Coming out of practice sessions he was besieged by media people. Television cameras and tape recorders were stuck in his face.

The hounding seemed endless.

Molvina gave quiet assurance that she would stand by whatever decision Ron made. Biff Poggi telephoned to give his support. Ron set aside two hours to be alone to sort through his desires and emotions in order to determine God's will and plan.

First, he looked at it logically from the viewpoint of his career. Certainly, as the world judges success, the idea in the coaching profession is to be at the top of the heap. Some would do almost anything, to grasp what he was being offered. "Could it be a stepping stone to something even greater, as Bob Tankard and others think," he pondered.

"But how could I ever get greater national exposure than being at Nebraska—a team always ranked at the top? At Brown I'd be a bigger duck—but in a much smaller pond."

Judging the difference on that scale was impossible for him.

Ron was also faced with considerable pressure from some of the 220 members of the Black Coaches Association, of which he was an officer. Many saw this as a chance to break new ground. His steady response was, "I've been brought up to believe that being black doesn't mean being desperate. I need to make a prayerful decision based on wisdom, knowledge, and insight.

"The need now is for black coaches to have head positions where they can have sustained opportunities and the resources to win consistently."

Ron, from his earliest days, had an unyielding desire to help bridge the gap in race relations. He was already involved in that task as an assistant coach at Nebraska. One didn't have to go to the east coast to find racial tensions. Ron decided that this was not solely a decision based on racial factors.

During the early afternoon before the Cornhuskers' Fiesta Bowl practice, Ron threshed through his mind all the possibilities between going and staying. As he did so one word kept surfacing. That word was not success, of which he had been so enthralled as a young black boy from a modest home. Nor was it fame, of which he had dreamed as an aspiring athlete. No, the word pertained not to what he could gain but of what he could give. That word was ministry. During three short years in Lincoln, God had confirmed to Ron that his high profile position was given to him as a trust. He was to be a witness, to give expression to his faith in Jesus Christ. And to prove it, God had opened up amazing opportunities—all over America.

Ron chuckled to himself as he compared the extreme satisfaction of speaking in the name of Jesus to the dream of empty success which had haunted him just a few years earlier. He realized that he had not yearned to be a pro footballer just for the honor and opportunity: the quest for fame had been in neon as well.

Now, he was confronted with another opportunity which would afford him high prominence in his profession. The sports media was abuzz daily in anticipation of his decision. Most people were certain of what he would decide. Who wouldn't take hold of a head coaching position?

Ron Brown wouldn't!

In his search for peace in the matter he focused first on professional fact. He was a coach whether he stayed at Nebraska or returned to Providence. So what was the issue? To the mind of most people in the world, one must grab every chance to climb the ladder to success and recognition. Not to do so is folly.

However, Ron had an allegiance to a higher goal. His perspective for gauging life was centered in his personal responsibility as a child of God. He was to bear witness to the truth in Jesus Christ.

One significant opinion came from his friend, Ron Dickerson, another strong Christian, who at the time was defensive back coach at Penn State. His advice centered on a verse of Scripture, James 1:5

> If any of you lacks wisdom, he should ask
> God, who gives generously to all without finding
> fault, and it will be given to him.

"Listen, Ron," Dickerson declared, "close out everyone else's opinion and get God's wisdom—and stick to your guns."

Ron and Molvina proceeded to stay awake all night on December 29th, meditating on that verse and praying.

The next day he had his answer.

When he called John Parry, Athletic Director at Brown, with his decision, Parry was perplexed by the refusal, but he didn't pry for an explanation. As Ron made his surprise statement to the press that he was staying at Nebraska, those who are normally bursting with commentary were without words.

It was left to Ron to explain simply, "God has given me a real peace about staying as an assistant under Coach Osborne." Newsmen didn't want to get into a "Jesus" story, so they let the interview hang at that point.

Ron didn't expect people to necessarily understand his decision. In the final analysis it was too simple. A complex society wants mystery and intrigue. There was neither in Ron's story. He had found peace not in success but in service.

A couple of days later Ron received a letter from the father of David Seizys, a Nebraska player. Tony Seizys and Ron had grown to admire one another. Tony explained that he had not wanted to influence Ron's thinking, so he had waited until Ron made his final decision before sending him the letter. Tony shared a Bible verse which was to help Ron immensely in the following months of second guessing. It was John 6:27:

> Do not work for food that spoils, but for food
> that endures to eternal life, which the Son of Man
> will give you. On him God the Father has placed
> his seal of approval.

Ron was questioned daily by Nebraska fans; as well as college, pro, and high school coaches around the country about his decision to turn the Brown job down. Many just could not grasp it. Who, in a world bent on getting, can understand giving?

He smiled as he thought back through his own pilgrimage. "For years, like others, I couldn't have fathomed God's plan," he admitted. "But now I can!"

Subsequent events proved to confirm Ron's decision to stay at Nebraska. The opportunities to speak out on three matters of great concern to him multiplied: adoption, race relations, and the plight of underprivileged kids.

From the humble begining of the first "I CAN" camp at a rustic farm in South Carolina, Ron's desire to help low income kids has attracted support from many sources. Most striking of all was when the mayor of a nearby town drove out to a camp to see what was going on. He parked his car across the field and watched from a distance. He couldn't hear what was being said, but he saw what was being done with the kids. He then drove back into town and wrote out a check for $15,000 of his own money.

Requests come in for information on how to expand the camps to other areas. That poses one question for Ron and Biff Poggi as they see their vision expand: should they give in to the pressure to tone down the Gospel message in order to have even more camps?

Never!

"I'll never forget the first camp," Ron said with excitement to a reporter. "We had no idea what to expect. We didn't even know much about how to organize it. But the last night, as I shared my testimony as to how Christ transformed my life, every kid but one gave his life to Jesus.

"It was one of the most incredible experiences of my life. That's the real purpose of the camps. Sure we want kids to get a good grasp on life and a right attitude. But without Jesus Christ that's impossible."

Another pleasing opportunity for Ron was when he and his mother were able to do a television commercial together on the topic of adoption. It became even more important to him when he sat next to her hospital bed as she was waiting for bypass surgery.

They had plenty of time to reflect on their life together. His mother had often assured him and his sister that their birth mothers had loved them very much because they decided to give them life instead of death. That had to have been a difficult decision, but what an impact it had on so many lives.

Would Arthur and Pearl Brown have come to know Christ if they had not brought a club-footed child into their home? If he had been cut out of his mother's womb and thrown away like a piece of trash, would Victor Stachmus have had someone at his bedside to lead him into peace with God when he was so fearful of what lay beyond death?

But as Ron held his mother's hand that day he thought more of what was facing her at that moment. She asked him to read to her from the Psalms. When the orderly came to wheel her away to surgery, she assured her son, "I'm in the Lord's hands."

Her words were prophetic. The last he ever heard her utter. Pearl Brown never awoke from the surgery.

So is the life of Ron Brown. Basically a story about an insecure, weak person, who failed so often in his personal life, who had to say at one time, "I CAN'T", in order to achieve real success in life. Yet, one day, he allowed the blood of a Man named Jesus to erase that apostrophe "t" forever:

I CAN'T do all things through Christ who gives
me strength.

Philippians 4:13